CW00543754

TITANIC: 'ICEBERG AHEAD'

TITANIC: 'ICEBERG AHEAD'

The Story of the Disaster by Some of Those Who Were There

James W. Bancroft

FRONTLINE BOOKS

An imprint of
Pen & Sword Books Ltd

First published in Great Britain in 2021 by

Frontline Books
an imprint of Pen & Sword Books Ltd,
47 Church Street, Barnsley, S. Yorkshire, S70 2AS

ISBN 978 1 52677 206 0

A CIP catalogue record for this book is available from the British Library.

Typeset in Chennai, India
by Lapiz Digital Services.

For more information on our books, please visit
www.frontline-books.com, email info@frontline-books.com
or write to us at the above address.

Printed and bound by TJ Books Limited

Pen & Sword Books Ltd incorporates the imprints of Pen & Sword Archaeology, Atlas, Aviation, Battleground, Discovery, Family History, History, Maritime, Military, Naval, Politics, Social History, Transport, True Crime, Claymore Press, Frontline Books, Praetorian Press, Seaforth Publishing and White Owl

For a complete list of Pen & Sword titles please contact

PEN & SWORD BOOKS LTD
47 Church Street, Barnsley, South Yorkshire, S70 2AS, England
E-mail: enquiries@pen-and-sword.co.uk
Website: www.pen-and-sword.co.uk

Or

PEN AND SWORD BOOKS
1950 Lawrence Rd, Havertown, PA 19083, USA
E-mail: Uspen-and-sword@casematepublishers.com

Contents

PART I

Terror at Seven Bells

Introduction

The RMS *Titanic* disaster, which occurred on the night of 14/15 April 1912, is one of history's most catastrophic human tragedies and resulted in a terrible sacrifice of life. The people on board were proud to be part of the ship's maiden voyage, but what they didn't know was that it was destined to be its only voyage. It harbours many heartbreaking stories about its ill-fated passengers and crew, whose lives were painfully shattered by what they saw and experienced during that one dreadful incident.

RMS *Titanic* was a Liverpool-registered ocean liner built for the transatlantic passenger and Royal Mail service between Southampton and New York. She was constructed at the Harland and Wolff shipyard in Belfast and was launched on 31 May 1911. *Titanic* weighed over 46,000 tonnes and was valued at £1.5 million. She included sixteen watertight compartments featuring doors that could be closed automatically from the bridge, sealing off the compartments if necessary; the ship would still stay afloat even if four of the compartments were to flood. This system prompted White Star to describe the vessel as practically unsinkable.

She was the second of her class of luxury liners to be built, her slightly smaller sister ship, RMS *Olympic*, having sailed on her maiden voyage on 14 June 1911. *Titanic* was built to accommodate about 3,000 passengers and over 900 crew members, and being a Royal Mail ship, she was carrying about as many sacks of mail as people. *Titanic* had four funnels, although only three of them released steam from the boilers and one of them served no purpose other than the fact that the designers thought the ship would look more impressive with four funnels other than just three.

The ship was designed to provide the ultimate in luxury travel. There was a swimming pool with an adjacent Turkish bath suite, a state-of-the-art gymnasium, an à la carte restaurant, and the Café Parisien. However, the ship's main feature was the Grand Staircase. Built from solid English oak, and enhanced with wrought iron, the decorated glass domes above were designed to let in as much natural light as possible. To have sailed on 'the voyage of the century' aboard RMS *Titanic*, the world's largest and most luxurious vessel afloat at that time, was like being one of the first people to fly on Concorde. It was described at the time as 'a floating palace' – a combination of Mayfair and Bel Air on water!

However, for all its opulence, some members of the crew who had sailed on *Olympic* had expressed foreboding about that ship, and these apprehensive feelings did not fade when they transferred to *Titanic*. *Olympic* suffered several mishaps during her first months afloat. The most serious of these was when she collided with the British warship HMS *Hawke* on 20 September 1911, off the Isle of Wight, and had her hull badly damaged. In two further accidents she struck a sunken wreck and had to have a broken propeller replaced, and she nearly ran aground on one occasion while she was leaving Belfast. To get her back to service quickly after the damage, Harland and Wolff had to pull resources from *Titanic*, which fatefully delayed her maiden voyage by three weeks, from 20 March to 10 April.

In fact, fifty-three sailors were under arrest in Southampton because they had refused to sail to New York on *Olympic* unless that ship was fitted with wooden lifeboats instead of collapsible dinghies. They were found guilty of having refused duty. However, after what happened during *Titanic* disaster the magistrate decided that it was inexpedient to punish them.

In addition to these problems, there was serious industrial unrest at the time, and because of a coal strike some ships were unable to sail, so many of their passengers were transferred to *Titanic*.

Some strange bad omens came in the form of the written word long before *Titanic* was even thought of. On 22 March 1886, the well-known newspaper editor William Thomas Stead, a keen believer in spiritualism, who was fated to go down with *Titanic*, had published an article entitled: 'How the Mail Steamer went down in mid-Atlantic', by a Survivor, in which he wrote about a steamer that collides with another ship, and because of the shortage of lifeboats there is a large loss of life. He wrote 'This is exactly what might take place and will take place if liners are sent to sea short of boats – Ed'.

The White Star Line constructed a ship named *Majestic* and it was launched in 1889, and three years later an edition of W.T. Stead's magazine *Review of Reviews* carried a story entitled *From the Old World to the New*. Although the story was fictional, it was about a ship named *Majestic* of the

White Star Line that has set sail with a clairvoyant on board who senses a disaster to another ship that has collided with an iceberg. The survivors are rescued and the *Majestic* manages to avoid the ice.

In 1898 an American novelist named Morgan Andrew Robertson published a book entitled *Futility* or *The Wreck of the Titan*, about a fictional ocean liner that sank after hitting an iceberg and does not carry enough lifeboats for everyone on board. Both boats were roughly the same size, and they both sank 400 nautical miles from Newfoundland on an April evening. Although the fact and fictional similarities are uncanny, Robertson later stated that he did not have any psychic abilities, as his novel was based on his knowledge of shipbuilding and understanding of the dangers of modern shipping. He died less than three years after *Titanic* sank.

The fateful true-life omens continued to make things look bad. A fire broke out in the coal bunkers before *Titanic* had even left Belfast, which the trimmers and stokers below were desperately trying to get under control, and she almost collided with another large vessel as she was leaving the harbour at Southampton.

The delays and problems caused everything to be rushed, and to make up some of the lost time *Titanic* was steaming at a speed that the crews of other ships would have envied at the time. It was stated later that up to the moment the vessel struck the iceberg she had a speed of 22 knots an hour. Just before midnight on Sunday, 14 April 1912, the RMS *Titanic* began to send out signals of distress stating 'We have struck an iceberg'. It had collided with an enormous body of ice that stripped off her bilge under the waterline for more than a hundred yards, opened up five of the front compartments and flooded the coal bunker servicing one of the boilers. The ship that took three years to build took less than three hours to sink.

There were sixteen lifeboats and four collapsible dinghies, which were insufficient, as a consequence of which two out of every three people on board perished. It was one of the deadliest peacetime maritime disasters in modern history.

The CS *Carpathia* was on its way from New York to Gibraltar and fortunately the ship was in the region, and on receiving a distress signal from *Titanic* it immediately set a course towards the disaster area. After working through dangerous ice fields it arrived at the scene at four o'clock in the morning of 15 April. Some people, mostly women and children, had escaped from the ship in lifeboats and *Carpathia* saved over seven hundred of them.

Investigations into the tragedy took place soon after, with the US Senate beginning their inquiries less than a week after the tragedy, followed by the British Board of Trade inquiry later in the year. The overall findings stated a combination of failures that had led to the sinking. These included inadequate lifeboat facilities and regulations, and the fact that they were not filled to capacity when the ship was being abandoned; failure by the captain to take ice warnings seriously; and that the ship was travelling too fast in a minefield of dangerous waters.

Some people also suggested there were flaws in its design and construction. It is suspected that many of the bolts that held the vessel together were weak, and the bottom of the boat was not designed to withstand the weight of a major flooding. One passenger actually stated that the designer admitted the ship was not ready to sail when it did.

Consequently, the International Ice Patrol was set up and stricter regulations were introduced through the International Convention for the Safety of Life at Sea, both of which are still in place today. Maritime safety regulations were updated, including new lifeboat requirements, the introduction of lifeboat drills and the Radio Act of 1912, which insisted on twenty-four-hour communication access on passenger liners, and that communications concerning the safety of the ship took priority over passengers' personal messages. Of course, all these new regulations came too late for the poor unsuspecting passengers and crew who lost their lives.

The story of *Titanic* disaster is a record of many stories, and to study the lives of the people who were involved in the tragedy is like taking a step back in time; a paradigm of the Edwardian era. The remains of the wreck of RMS *Titanic* may lie on the bottom of a deep ocean, but its stories and legends will continue to surface forever, and people all over the world will continue to be interested in them.

I have tried to present the narrative in a way that allows the reader to make their own opinion about the main aspects of the disaster, and take the reader through the terrifying events as they unfolded, through the eyes of a selection of people who experienced them and left descriptions of what they saw and suffered; with biographical tributes giving information on the type of people they were and what happened in later life for those who survived.

*Where a name is accompanied by an asterisk a biographical tribute appears in Part II.

1. 'Health and Safety?'

White Star Line had become involved in a competition with their rivals, the Cunard Line, over the immensely lucrative Atlantic passenger trade. It was a fight in which size and luxury really mattered. White Star's president, J Bruce Ismay, intended to get ahead so he came up with plans to build three new ships that would be better than Cunard's – and they would be called *Olympic, Titanic* and *Britannic.*

The Blue Riband was an unofficial accolade given to passenger liners in regular service that crossed the Atlantic Ocean in the fastest speed, usually from Queenstown in Southern Ireland to Sandy Nook in New Jersey. It was recognised for the fastest speed westbound and also for the eastbound journey. Since the turn of the century it had been held by German double-screw steamers. However, the Cunard Line took over the record in both directions after the launch of their large liners *Lusitania* on 7 June 1906, and *Mauretania* on 20 September 1906.

Lusitania took the westbound record during its trip of 6 to 10 October 1907, when it reached a speed of 23.99 knots (44.43 km/h). The ship increased the record three times, reaching a speed of 25.65 knots (47.50 km/h) on its trip of 8 to 12 August 1909. *Mauretania* gained the record during its trip of 26 to 30 September 1909, when it reached a speed of 26.06 knots (48.26 km/h). That record would stand for twenty years.

Lusitania took the eastbound record with a speed of 23.61 knots (43.73 km/h) during its trip on 19 to 24 October 1907. This was fractionally beaten by *Mauretania* on its 30 November to 5 December 1907 trip, when it reached a speed of 23.69 knots (43.87 km/h). However, the ship increased the record six times, reaching a speed of 25.88 knots (47.93 km/h) during its trip of 16 to 21 June 1909. This record stood until *Mauretania* itself beat it fifteen years later.

White Star had last held the westbound record with *Teutonic* in 1891, and it had not held the eastbound record since the old *Britannic* as far back as 1876.

When information concerning Ismay's plans became public, and the news that the new ships would be built at Harland and Wolff in Belfast, the local press lauded 'There is great satisfaction in Belfast of the prospect of assured work for a considerable period being given by the building of two mammoth White Star liners. It is estimated that at least £2,000,000 will be spent in wages in Belfast. Twelve thousand men are employed in Messrs Harland and Wolff's shipyards, the wages bill reaching £18,000 a week.'

Olympic was ordered in 1907 to be built at yard number SS400. Several men working on the construction of *Olympic* had lost their lives, including Robert Murphy junior, whose father was to meet his death while involved in the building of the other great ship. The first two men to suffer accidental death in the construction of *Titanic* at Queen's Island were young teenagers, and strangely each known man who met his death during construction was older than the one who had been killed before him.

On 20 April 1910, a fifteen-year-old named Samuel Joseph Scott said goodbye to his family, left their lodgings at 70 Templemore Street in the Ballymacarret district of east Belfast and joined the other workers as they made their way down to 'The Yard'. He was a catch boy working on the ship then known simply as SS401. His job was to climb a high ladder to a platform where white hot rivets were thrown up to him and he had to catch them with a pair of tongues. He would then hold them in a hole ready for one of the five-man team of riveters to drive them home with a heavy hammer.

That afternoon he was busy at his work when perhaps he had to stretch out a bit too far to catch a rivet and he somehow lost his footing and fell helplessly for 23ft onto the hard surface of the ship's hull, where he lay bleeding from a serious head trauma. The cause of death was given as 'shock, following a fracture to the skull'. Sam was buried in an unmarked grave at Belfast City Cemetery on the Falls Road, and eight other men lost their lives during the construction of SS401, which would later be named RMS *Titanic*.

Just over two months later, on 23 June 1910, another teenage rivet catcher suffered the same fate. John Kelly was aged 19 and lived in Convention Street. He too died from shock after he fell from a great height. He was laid to rest in an unmarked grave not far from where Sam is buried.

On 17 November 1910, a twenty-seven-year-old driller named William Clarke was injured in an accident. He was taken to the Royal Victoria Hospital, where he died of broncopneumonia. Bill lived at 35 Comber Street in Belfast.

On 31 May 1911, workers watched with great pride as *Titanic* slid down the slipways from her building berth and splashed into the waters of Victoria Channel in Belfast Harbour.

A young lad named John Parkinson watched with emotion as the great liner was launched because Frank, his father, had worked on the ship. He said to his dad 'How can a ship that big stay on the water?' to which Frank replied confidently 'Johnny; that ship will always stay up in the water!'

Forty-three-year-old shipwright James Dobbin was responsible for looking after the giant chains and wooden props that held *Titanic* secure on the slipway. As the great ship moved and the greased stanchions that had been helping to keep her in place fell away, Jim was completely unaware that one of them was falling his way, or he did not have a chance to get out of the way when he realised the danger, but his body was crushed as timbers piled on top of him. The official cause of death was 'shock and haemorrhage following a fracture of the pelvis'. Jim lived at 13 Memel Street in Belfast, was married to Rachel and had a seventeen-year-old son named James, who was an apprentice plumber at the shipyard.

Another worker named Bob Murphy had lost his son and namesake in a tragic accident while he was working on the building of *Olympic*. Bob worked as a rivet counter, and on 13 June 1911, just after the hooter had sounded for the end of the shift at six o'clock, he stopped work for the day and was making his way across a plank gangway on one of the upper decks about 50ft above the ground when the boards suddenly parted. Taken by surprise, Bob lost his footing and fell heavily onto a metal tank top. He was rushed to the Royal Victoria Hospital in an ambulance, but he died from shock following a compound fracture to the base of his skull.

Robert James Murphy was aged fifty-nine and lived at 6 Hillman Street in the New Lodge district of Belfast. He was laid to rest in the burial ground of Carnmoney Parish Church, Glengormley, Newtownabbey. He was the last known man to be killed while working on the building of *Titanic*, although three other men are believed to have lost their lives but their names were never recorded. It was considered to be a low casualty count in comparison to the vast labour force employed at the yard, the unprecedented scope of the project, and the almost non-existent safety codes.

Nevertheless, there were obvious plans to extend the production of large sea-going liners, as the *London Financial News* reported in early April 1912, under the heading 'Dry Docks for Big Liners':

> The recent successful dry-docking of the giant White Star liner *Titanic* at Belfast is a timely reminder of the fact that no other port in the world could find such accommodation for her. Not only so, but the harbour commissioners there are taking steps for the purpose of enlarging their Alexandra Dock, where the *Titanic* is lying, so as to provide room for even bigger vessels. The Trafalgar Dock at Southampton will be large enough when the alterations are completed, and provision is being made for mammoth liners on the Clyde and the Mersey; but, so far as is known, nowhere else. And of dry docks abroad there are only three which could accommodate a ship of the *Lusitania* class. In this connection it is interesting to note that, notwithstanding the importance of trans-Atlantic traffic, there are no fewer than 18 steamers trading to New York which cannot be docked anywhere in the United States.

Titanic disaster was not the only one to occur in 1912. On 11 March that year the *Daily Chronicle* reported that the Norwegian explorer Roald Amundsen had reached the South Pole on 14 December 1911. Before his party left for home they had erected their national flag. Subsequent news reports told how the expedition of Captain Robert Falcon Scott had reached the South Pole on 18 January 1912, only to discover they had been beaten to their objective. Beset by hardships during their return journey, Petty Officer Edgar Evans died of exhaustion, and soon afterwards the four survivors became held up by a furious blizzard. On 17 March Captain Lawrence Oates, who was suffering with frostbite and gangrene, left their tent and walked to his death, with the immortal sentence: 'I am just going outside, and may be some time.' It was his thirty-second birthday. Scott and his two remaining companions, Lieutenant Henry 'Birdy' Bowers and Doctor Edward Wilson, died later, the last entry in Scott's diary being written on 29 March.

It is interesting to note that Captain Scott's wife, Kathleen, who was a sculptor, was working on a memorial statue to Captain Edward Smith when news of the fate of her husband's expedition reached Britain. She would later be commissioned to produce a memorial statue of her husband in New Zealand, and one depicting Doctor Edward Wilson in Cheltenham.

2. 'All Aboard!'

The chief designer of the RMS *Titanic* was an Irishman named Thomas Andrews*, who made a point of sailing with a team of mechanics on the maiden voyages of many of his ships, including *Adriatic*, *Oceanic* and *Olympic*. *Titanic* would be no different. He left his wife and daughter in Belfast to embark for the liner's initial trip to Southampton, and then on to America. Some members of the crew also embarked at Belfast on 25 March 1912, and as they travelled with it they were tasked to get the ship prepared for the journey across the Atlantic Ocean.

Billy 'Punch' Wynn* had already been involved in two maritime emergencies and two wars when he joined the White Star Line in 1902, where he was assigned to *Oceanic*. He was living in Southampton, and as the quartermaster he was given new instructions: 'One day the men were assembled, and I was chosen to proceed to Belfast, where I found I was posted to *Titanic*.'

The ship arrived at Southampton during the first hour of 4 April 1912, and by midday men were turning up at the dock to sign on as members of the crew. A typical individual among them was Sam Webb*, who had left his job in a colliery to work on *Olympic*, and like hundreds of others he transferred to *Titanic* for her maiden voyage. Because of this the only drill that took place while the vessel was docked at Southampton, or indeed during the voyage, consisted of lowering two lifeboats on the starboard side into the water, and these boats were again hoisted to the boat deck within half an hour. No boat list was posted that clearly designated where members of the crew should be stationed in the event of an emergency until several days after sailing from Southampton, and few knew their proper stations until the following Friday morning.

Titanic made a majestic sight as she was moored for five days in berth 43 at Dock Gate 4, the entrance to the Eastern Dock in Southampton. People from all walks of life began embarking on her on 10 April 1912, for what was to be the trip of a lifetime. Many were looking forward to starting new lives in the United States. In 1912 class distinction was reluctantly tolerated by most people, and all three classes of accommodation on *Titanic* were segregated by doors and barriers, and the passengers would not enter in an area that was not of their class.

Married couples and families with children in first- and second-class cabins were allowed to stay together, but in third class all male and female passengers were separated in different cabins. The men and older sons had to sleep in cabins at the bow of the ship, while women, older daughters and young children had to stay in accommodation at the stern.

It was known that sailors and the crews of ships were superstitious and sometimes harboured bad forebodings about their coming voyages, and frequently the bad feelings proved to be true. For instance, a sailor named William Marshfield of the Royal Navy left an account about one particular let-off he had:

> I am a superstitious man, a man with what are called presentiments. Everybody knows what presentiments are, but no one has ever been able to explain them. You are overwhelmed with a sense of coming evil – that is what presentiment means.
>
> In the early part of 1870 I was drafted to HMS *Captain*. From the moment that order was given I was so filled with a foreboding of disaster that I went to the length of vowing that rather than go to sea in the ship I would leave the service. It was no good reasoning with or laughing at me; it was useless to say that the *Captain* was designed by a famous man, and that he himself had so much faith in the vessel that he was going to sea in her. I refused to be laughed or talked out of my forgiving, and at last, by a stroke of luck, I got transferred to HMS *Excellent*, gunnery ship.
>
> The *Captain* sailed a few months afterwards, and during the night capsized in the Bay of Biscay, carrying with her nearly all her officers and men, as well as her confiding designer. Only the watch on deck, less than a score of souls, was saved.

It would seem that Seaman Marshfield was somewhat unlucky, as he was boatswain on HMS *Calliope* when it had to be rescued during a hurricane off Samoa in 1889, and again during the loss of HMS *Victoria* when it was rammed and sunk in the Mediterranean Sea in 1893.

The unhappy first marriage of Able Seaman Joe Scarrott* had resulted in him committing bigamy, although neither of the women in his life was aware of it. He stated how he was reluctant to go on the journey right up until the ship actually left the dock:

I signed on the 'articles as 'A B' on Monday, 8 April 1912. The signing on seemed like a dream to me, and I could not believe I had done so, but the absence of my discharge book from my pocket convinced me. When we went to the docks that morning I had so much intention of applying for a job on the Big 'Un as we called her, as I had of going for a trip to the moon. I was assured of as job as Q M on a Union Castle liner … When I went home [36 Albert Road] and told my sister [Elizabeth] what I had done she called me a … fool. Now, this was the first and only time that she had shown disapproval of any ship I was going on. In fact, she would not believe me until she found I was minus my discharge book.

I was under orders to join the ship at 7 am, Wednesday, 10 April, the time of sailing being 12:00 that morning. It was to be a 'speed up' trip, meaning that we were to go from Southampton to New York, unload, load and back again in 16 days. Although it was unnecessary to take all my kit for this short trip, I did not seem to have the inclination to sort any of it out, and I pondered a lot in my mind whether I should (board) her or give it a miss. Now, in the whole of my 29 years of going to sea I have never had that feeling of hesitation that I experienced then, and I had worked aboard *Titanic* when she came to Southampton from the builders, and I had the opportunity to inspect her from stem to stern. This I did, especially the crew quarters, and I must say that she was the finest ship I had ever seen.

On Wednesday 10th, I decided to go, but not with a good heart. Before leaving home I kissed my sister and said 'Goodbye', and as I was leaving she called me back and asked why I had said 'Goodbye' instead of my usual, 'So long, see you again soon.'

On my way to join the ship you can imagine how this incident stuck in my mind. On joining a ship all sailors have much the same routine. You go to your quarters, choose your bunk, and get the gear you require from your bag. Then you change into your uniform. By that time you are called to muster by the chief officer. I took my bag but did not open it, nor did I get into uniform, and I went to muster and fire and boat drill without my uniform. 11:45 am. Hands to stations for casting off. I am in the starboard watch,

> my station is aft, and I am still not in uniform. My actions and manners are the reverse of what they should be. 12:00 noon the order to let go is given.

Chief baker Charles Joughin* had previously served on *Olympic* and he was of the opinion 'It was practically a crew from the *Olympic*'.

George Barlow* was born at Salford in 1872. He was in Southampton to sign on as a first-class bedroom steward. The cabin or bedroom stewards were employed with keeping rooms tidy and ready for passengers, and all other types of room service, including carrying luggage to rooms when a guest first arrives. In addition to cleaning the rooms, keeping beds tidy, replacing towels, and other basic services, the cabin steward also provides information to guests and help to improve their experiences on the ship. All employees on a ship should be trustworthy, but as a cabin steward is often in a passenger's room, these employees must be particularly friendly, honest, professional, and polite. They are usually responsible for the upkeep of a set of rooms, most often in the same general area.

Like numerous members of *Titanic* crew, George had served on *Olympic*, which was said to be an unlucky vessel, being referred to as a 'ghost ship'. George's father said that when his son was serving as a steward on *Olympic* he was 'frightened' of her, and said 'many times' that he was sure she would sink.

Tom Whiteley* was a Mancunian, described by a newspaper as 'an intelligent young fellow … with light hair and blue eyes'. He had just celebrated his eighteenth birthday on 3 April. He too had previously served on *Olympic* as a steward in the first-class dining saloon. According to the newspaper report, Tom had a foreboding that misfortune would overtake the vessel. Bidding goodbye to some friends at Southampton, he is said to have remarked 'I don't think I shall ever see you again. We are going to have a wreck.'

Stewardess Violet Jessop* had transferred from *Olympic*. Violet was a devout Roman Catholic, and she always carried a rosary on her person, believing strongly in the power of prayer. She had brought on board a copy of a translated Hebrew prayer that an old Irish woman had given to her, which was supposed to protect her from fire and water. Stewardesses worked as much as seventeen hours a shift and were among the lowest paid on the ship.

Chief Officer Henry Wilde wrote a letter to his sister in which he stated 'I don't like this ship. I have a queer feeling about it.'

Esther Hart*, her husband, Benjamin*, and their seven-year-old daughter, Eva*, had travelled down from Essex on the boat train. Ben's carpentry business was not doing too well, so they planned to travel to Winnipeg in Canada 'Where I'll either sink or swim!' – as Ben put it. He intended to start building with a Mr Wire. They were originally booked on SS *Philadelphia*, but Ben changed his plans because he wanted to visit a relative in New York while he had the chance and therefore they transferred to *Titanic*. Esther described Eva as being 'very bonny', and that 'everybody takes notice of her ... the teddy bear'.

Esther was already concerned that they were leaving behind her father and mother, who were quite old and not in the best of health. She had never had any kind of premonitions before, but she considered all the talk of the ship being unsinkable was flying in the face of God, and she stated 'I can honestly say that from the moment the journey to Canada was mentioned till the time we got aboard *Titanic* I never contemplated with any other feelings but those of dread and uneasiness'.

Arthur Gee* was a Salfordian in his late-forties. He was the son of a calico dyer, and he had studied the chemistry of calico printing in Germany. A multi-linguist, he had apparently organised the trip across the Atlantic to take a job as manager of a linen mill near Mexico City, after which he was contemplating retiring. His first-class ticket cost him nearly £40.

He intended to sail from Liverpool, but because industrial unrest had affected the port there the ship was delayed and, as fate would have it, he happily agreed to travel to Southampton to board the brand new luxury liner RMS *Titanic*.

His dog had acted strangely on the day he made his way to the station, as if it sensed foreboding and was trying to warn him not to get on the train. His local newspaper at Lytham in Lancashire reported:

> He kept a dog, which usually reserved its most affectionate demonstrations for Mr Gee's children. Mr Gee, in the course of his business, made frequent journeys from home, but his going and comings were apparently regarded with unconcern by the dog. On the occasion of his departure to embark at Southampton, however, the dog followed the cab to the railway station, and at the station jumped about Mr Gee in so demonstrative a fashion that he remarked on the strangeness of the incident to a friend who was

> seeing him off, and said how remarkable it was that the dog should appear to know that he was going on a long voyage.

Arthur was obviously impressed by the ship, and in a letter written on White Star Line stationary while the ship was docked at Queenstown, he told his wife:

> In the language of the poet, 'this is a knock-out.' I have never seen anything so magnificent, even in a first class hotel. I might be living in a palace. It is, indeed, an experience. We seem to be miles above the water, and there are certainly miles of promenade deck. The lobbies are so long that they appear to come to a point in the distance. Just finished dinner. They call us up to dress by bugle. It reminded me of some Russian villages where they call the cattle home from the fields by horn made from the bark of a tree. Such a dinner! My gracious!

Henry Forbes Julian* described his accommodation as 'more like a small bedroom than a ship's cabin.' Lizzie Bonnell* was a spinster in her sixty-second year. She had been living in Southport since 1896, where she was involved in a number of local political, religious and social organisations. She was sailing to America on a first-class ticket to see members of her family, and was travelling with several people, including her niece, Caroline Bonnell. Caroline kept a diary, and on 9 April she wrote:

> Dear Diary, I am writing this as I pack for my trip across the Atlantic Ocean with my Aunt Elizabeth. We will also be accompanied by the Wick family. As a thirty-year-old, I am grateful to be going on this trip, as we are boarding the ship at Southampton. I was over here in Europe when I met up with two very nice men named Washington Roebling and Stephen Weart Blackwell; they will also be travelling on *Titanic*.
>
> I've heard that the ship is very luxurious, and my parents, John Meek Bonnell and Emily Wick, only expect the best. Yesterday, I got word that I will be sharing a cabin with another girl of the Wick family. I will be staying in cabin C-7, so close to the main

> deck, with Mary Natalie Wick. I am a first class passenger, so I'm expecting the best from this 'unsinkable' beauty! Hopefully nothing bad should happen, and I won't get lonely with all the company I have. I must get to packing, I don't want to lose my ticket; the print on the ticket is just so elegant … I can't wait!

The *Southport Guardian* noted:

> Miss Lizzie Bonnell was going with a niece on one of her frequent visits to a brother in the States, and only on Sunday evening 'Miss Jennie' of Day Nursery fame, was telling me of a letter her sister had sent from Southampton describing the luxurious comfort of her roomy cabin and all the splendid arrangements on board, and saying that she thought this would be the pleasantest trip she had ever made.

Marian Meanwell* was a sixty-three-year-old Lancastrian divorcee. She was supposed to have sailed on *Majestic* to see her daughter in America, but when she arrived in Southampton she was happy to accept a transfer onto the brand-new luxury liner *Titanic*, which was to replace the *Majestic* on the cross-Atlantic service. Although she was carrying a crocodile skin handbag that was decorated with brightly coloured jewels, she had only £3 in the bank and a third-class ticket in her purse. Soon after seeing *Titanic* she sent a letter to her cousin stating 'I am delighted with *Titanic*. In my view, nothing approaching the accommodation has been experienced in any of the previous journeys and nothing but a pleasant voyage is anticipated.'

Benjamin Howard* was a retired railway worker from Swindon, who was travelling with his wife Ellen to visit their sons in America. Their daughter, Ethel, told a local newspaper:

> They left home by the 2:15pm train to Southampton on Tuesday, and set sail on *Titanic* on the Wednesday. I had been thinking of going to Southampton to see them off, but I did not do so.
>
> We had a postcard from Cherbourg, and only on Friday night a letter from Queenstown. A very nice letter too. But we little thought that this was the last we should hear of them.

Adolf Saalfeld* was of Jewish descent, born in Germany in 1865. He moved to England when he was about twenty years old, and as a self-made businessman he became the chairman of a chemist's merchants in Manchester. He boarded *Titanic* at Southampton as a first-class passenger; his cabin being on C Deck, and opposite the cabin of John Jacob Astor VI, the wealthiest man on board.

He was very impressed by the ship, and before boarding he and his nephew-in-law, Paul, toured the ship together. He wrote to his wife, Gertrude, on 10 April on White Star Line's stationery imprinted with the words: 'On board RMS Titanic', which may be the very first letter written on the ship by an early-boarding passenger, stating 'I just had an hour's roaming about on this wonderful boat together with Paul. I like my cabin very much. It is like a bed-sitting room and rather large. I am the first man to write a letter on board, they are still busy to finish the last touches on board.'

After saying goodbye to Adolphe, Paul wrote a letter to his wife, which stated 'Uncle has a very large cabin, nearly a living room with a sofa and an electric ventilator'.

After setting sail, Adolphe followed this up by remarking of his journey:

> ... approval of a luncheon featuring soup, fillet of plaice, a loin chop with cauliflower and fried potatoes.'
>
> The weather is calm and fine, the sky overcast. There are only 370 First Class passengers. So far the boat does not move and goes very steadily. It is not nice to travel alone and leave you behind. I think you will have to come next time.
>
> I had a long promenade and a doze for an hour up to 5 o'clock. The band played in the afternoon for tea, but I savour a coffee in the veranda cafe with bread and butter, and quite thought that I should have to pay, but anything and everything in the eating line is gratis.

A young boy aged about four years old, who was known as 'Lolo', was travelling with his father, Louis Hofmann, and his younger brother, who was known as Momon. However, his father was keeping a closely guarded secret from the other passengers. In later life Lolo described *Titanic* as:

> A magnificent ship! I remember looking down the length of the hull – the ship looked splendid. My brother and I played on the

> forward deck and were thrilled to be there. One morning my father, my brother and I were eating eggs in the second class dining room. The sea was stunning. My feeling was one of total and utter well-being.

There was an even darker secret being kept from the knowledge of the passengers, in the form of a raging fire that had broken out in coal bunker number 6, and which the firemen below were desperately trying to keep under control.

Men would receive £6 a month for working as firemen/stokers in the engine room, where their duties included feeding the furnaces with coal brought to them by trimmers. There were twenty-nine boilers, which powered the three massive engines. The men who worked in this department were known as the 'Black Gang' because of their dirty appearance, and they were rarely seen by the passengers.

Titanic's bunkers were set up so that trimmers did not need to wheel the coal to the firemen as they did in some other ships. There was a bunker door opposite each boiler, so that the firemen could just turn around and scoop up the coal. Trimmers were still needed to haul away the ash from the boilers. About once a watch the ash would be pulled out of each furnace and dumped on the plates in front of the boiler. The trimmer had to cool the ash with a hose and cart it to the ash ejectors, where it was fired into the sea by a high-pressure jet of water. Trimmers were also needed to remove coal from remote parts of the bunkers and keep the supply near the bunkers full.

There were four trimmers in each boiler room, one fireman for each of the ten boiler ends, and a leading fireman in overall charge of the boiler room. All the boiler rooms were supervised by a senior engineer. Each fireman had three furnaces to tend and it was hard but skilled work. It was a lot more than just shovelling coal, and a good experienced fireman could use half the coal of an unskilled man, and many had learned to keep the doors closed because of the intense heat.

Even the seventeen greasers who lubricated the engines on *Titanic* had a daunting task. Imagine a block of metal the size of a car engine revolving so quickly that you can't even follow it with your eye; then imagine trying to stroke it as it flits by with a rag full of grease.

Leading Fireman Fred Barrett* was a Liverpudlian, with much experience on several ships, including the SS *New York*. He reported:

> Just after departure from Southampton I and about ten other men received orders to empty the coal bunker in boiler room six, where a fire had been discovered. It took them three days to get it under control, and when Fred went back to see the extent of the damage he noted that the bulkhead was damaged from top to bottom, the lower half being warped at the back and the upper half being warped at the front.

Fireman/Stoker John Dilley*, an ex-army man whose real name was Christopher Shulver, was extremely light-fingered and had many brushes with the London police, which is probably why he had used a false name when he signed on:

> From the day we sailed *Titanic* was on fire, in bunker 6, and my sole duty, together with eleven other men, had been to fight that fire. We had made no headway against it.
>
> Of course the passengers knew nothing of the fire. There were hundreds of tons of coal stored there. The coal on top of the bunker was wet, as all of the coal should have been, but down at the bottom of the bunker the coal was dry. The coal at the bottom of the bunker took fire and smouldered for days. The wet coal on the top kept the flames from coming through, but down in the bottom of the bunker the flames were raging …
>
> Two men from each watch of stokers were told off to fight the fire. The stokers worked four hours at a time, so 12 of us were fighting the flames from the day we put out of Southampton till we hit the iceberg.

Chief engineer Joseph Bell* was the son of Cumbrian farmers, who had served part of his apprenticeship with the firm established by the famous engineer Robert Stephenson in Newcastle. He was superintending the work to keep the fire in check, when a second disaster was averted as the ship was leaving the harbour. As *Titanic* was passing Fireman Barrett's old ship, the liner SS *New York*, itself a very large vessel, the swell of water made by the propellers of the massive ship caused the *New York* to snap all seven hawsers that were securing it to the dock and its stern drifted quickly out towards *Titanic*. It was within a few yards of a collision when Captain Smith ordered

'Astern!' and *Titanic*'s tugboat got the hawsers on it just in time and got it back under control. It was not a good omen for the passengers and crew. Joe wrote a letter to his son and posted it at Queenstown on 11 April, in which he stated:

> We have made a good run from Southampton, everything working A1. We nearly had a collision with the *New York* and the *Oceanic* when leaving Southampton. The wash of our propellers made the two ships range about when we were passing them. This made their mooring ropes break and the *New York* set off across the river until the tugs got hold of her again. No damage was done but it looked like trouble at the time.

John Butterworth* had also worked on the *New York*, and he wrote a letter to his wife from Queenstown:

> We have been having a very fierce time in this steamer. I suppose you heard of the accident that occurred to the *New York* as we sailed. This ship carried so much water between the *Oceanic* and *New York* that the *York* broke all her ropes and sailed all on her own, you could have tossed a penny from our ship to her she was close, it was a good job she did not hit us as it would have been another case of the *Hawke* collision.

Leonard Taylor* was working at Derby Baths in Blackpool as a masseur when he answered an ad in the local newspaper asking for people to work on *Titanic*, so he applied for and gained a position in the Turkish Bath room. He wrote a letter home to his parents in which he stated:

> Dear Father and mother, I am on the briny ocean and nearing Queenstown, we passed Cherbourg last night. I suppose you read about our narrow escape when coming out of the Docks at Southampton. The suction power of the propellers was so great that she broke loose another vessel lying outside port, and was only a hair's breadth from hitting her. I am very comfortable – getting good food and good bunk, my wages are low but I will let you know all later as I want to catch the Queenstown mail. I am only writing

> to let you know I am all right. I will write next week sending full particulars about my non-too-good job. Well, goodbye. I shall come home after the trip as it is cheaper. They issue tickets at £1. PS – The boats rocking around.

Adolphe Saalfeld related:

> After leaving at noon we had quite a little excitement, as the tremendous suction of the steamer made all the hawsers of the SS *New York* snap as we passed her and she drifted on to our boat, a collision being averted by our stopping, and our tugs coming to the rescue of the *New York*.

Young Albert Ervine* was an electrician working on the top of the back funnel of *Titanic* with his friend, Alfred Middleton, and they both had a good panoramic view of the incident. He wrote a letter to his mother while he was on his way from Cherbourg to Queenstown and posted it when he arrived. It showed that he had complete confidence in the ship, but it contained a somewhat poignant last line:

> Yours received at Cherbourg, France, yesterday evening. We have had everything working nicely so far, except when leaving Southampton.
>
> As soon as *Titanic* began to move out of the dock, the suction caused the *Oceanic*, which was alongside her berth, to swing outwards, while another liner *(New York)* broke loose altogether and bumped into the *Oceanic*. The gangway of the *Oceanic* simply dissolved.
>
> Middleton and myself were on the top of the aft funnel, so we saw everything quite distinctly. I thought there was going to be a proper smash up owing to the high wind; but I don't think anyone was hurt.
>
> Well, we were at Cherbourg last night. It was just a mass of fortifications. We are on our way to County Cork. The next call then is New York.

> I am on duty morning and evening from 8 to 12; that is four hours work and eight hours off (have just been away attending the alarm bell).
>
> This morning we had a full dress rehearsal of an emergency. The alarm bells all rang for ten seconds, then about 50 doors, all steel, gradually slid down into their places, so that water could not escape from one section to the next.
>
> So you see it would be impossible for the ship to be sunk in collision with another.

Adolph Saalfeld stated:

> At 6 o'clock we anchored outside Cherbourg and two tugs with passengers came alongside. Owing to our little mishap at Southampton we were all an hour late and had dinner only at 7:30 instead of 7 o'clock as usual.
>
> After a fair night's rest and an excellent breakfast I am enjoying a promenade in glorious weather. The wind is fresh and the sea moderate, but on this big boat one hardly notices any movement. I write these lines just before we are getting into Queenstown so that you get them tomorrow morning. I shall not be able to write to you again before getting to New York.
>
> PS: Shall write to office on arrival and Eric will no doubt phone you at once.

Thomas Andrews wrote a note from Cherbourg to his wife:

> We reached here in nice time and took on board quite a number of passengers. The two little tenders looked well; you will remember we built them about a year ago. We expect to arrive at Queenstown about 10:30am tomorrow. The weather is fine and everything shaping for a good voyage. I have a seat at the doctor's table.

As the ship sailed across the English Channel, Joe Scarrott accepted that he had no choice but to get over his grim premonitions:

> Our first port of call was Cherbourg, and before we arrived there I had resigned myself to the inevitable and had settled down to my proper routine. After embarking continental passengers and mails we left for Queenstown, which was our last call before crossing the Atlantic, which we hoped to do at record speed.

Another Irish teenager named Jeremiah Burke boarded at Queenstown with his cousin, Honora Hegarty. He had with him a bottle of holy water that had been given to him for good luck on the voyage. It seems that he emptied the bottle and placed inside it a piece of paper on which he had written the date of 10 April 1912, and the words: 'From Titanic. Good Bye *(sic)* all. Burke of Glanmire, Cork.'

There were many stories of people who should have travelled on *Titanic* but for various reasons they did not do so and had a lucky escape.

Guglielmo Marconi, the man who had invented the wireless equipment that was used on *Titanic*, had been offered a free passage on the ship, but he decided to travel on *Lusitania* instead.

The London Symphony Orchestra had planned to sail on *Titanic* on their way to a three-week tour of the United States and Canada. However, the tour was rescheduled to begin at an earlier date and they travelled on board the SS *Baltic* during the previous week.

An American passenger named Charles Moore had planned to transport as many as a hundred English foxhounds on *Titanic*, with the intention of starting an English-style fox hunt, but he made arrangements for them to travel on a different vessel at the last minute.

3. The Hands of Fate

The ship eventually got out into open water and began its voyage westward, surging relentlessly through the waves and across the north Atlantic trying to make up for the time it had lost – and also the race for the westbound Blue Riband was on. Most people were thrilled with anticipation at the prospect of a new, exciting future as the rapidly prospering United States of America awaited them. Few passengers harboured foreboding, and it is likely that as they looked around and admired the opulence they would find reassurance in the thought that the designers and builders would not have gone through so much trouble to make it all so grand and luxurious if they thought for one moment that it could possibly sink.

However, Esther Hart still had no faith in the ship no matter how big and fancy it was. Her forebodings caused her to be particularly wary of how the ship was performing, and she was not convinced when she had been told that it was so big that it was not supposed to roll badly as it pounded through the waves. She slept during the day and stayed awake at night, seemingly presuming if there was going to be a problem it would happen during the dark hours. She wrote:

> Anyhow it rolls enough for me, I shall never forget it. It is nice weather but awfully windy and cold. They say we may get into New York Tuesday night but we were really due early on Wednesday morning. The sailors say we have had a wonderful passage, up to now there has been no tempest, but God knows what it must be like when there is one. This rough expanse of water, no land in sight and the ship rolling from side to side is very wonderful though they say this ship does not roll on account of its size. We have met some nice people on board and so it has been nice so far. But oh the long, long days and nights. It's the longest week I ever spent in my life.

Thomas Andrews was of the opinion that all was shipshape and Bristol fashion:

> Today I made my usual inspection of the ship. I talked to a few people on the deck and then went around the ship to see if there was anyone who could use a little help … No problems of great importance have risen so far. As passengers are starting to get comfortable in the ship there has been less for me to do. So far, it's been a delightful cruise for everyone.

Tommie was very popular with the crew, and during the voyage chief baker Charles Joughin prepared a special loaf of bread for him. He spent most of the voyage making notes on things to improve about the ship and its facilities. He usually dined on the next table to an American woman named Eleanor Cassebeer, and she later stated that Tommie had mentioned to her that 'The vessel was started on her maiden voyage before she was finished'. However, he also stated that the ship was 'as nearly perfect as human brains can make her'.

Harry Etches* was the bedroom steward stationed at the aft portside of Deck B, where he was in charge of eight cabins, including that of the mining tycoon Benjamin Guggenheim, B-84, and one cabin on A Deck (A-36) belonging to Thomas Andrews. He stated:

> Every morning at seven I went to his cabin. I would take him some fruit and tea. I used to see him again when he dressed at night. That would be a quarter or twenty minutes to seven, as a rule. He was rather late in dressing. I had met him several times at Belfast because I had been on the *Olympic*.

Many passengers took regular strolls along the promenades after dinner. It is likely that some of them became aware that there did not seem to be enough lifeboats for the vast number of people on board the ship and they expressed concern at what would happen if there was a reason to have to evacuate. But they were consoled by the fact that they were on board the unsinkable *Titanic*.

There were fourteen standard wood lifeboats measuring 30ft long by 9ft wide, with a capacity of sixty-five persons. There were two wood cutter 'emergency' lifeboats. They were both just over 7ft wide, with one being just over 25ft long and the other 2ft short. Both had a capacity of forty people. There were four Englehardt collapsible boats, which were about 27½ft long and 8ft broad, with a capacity of forty-seven persons. If anyone knew the details and did the maths they would realise that the total capacity was 1,178 souls, not even half the people on board.

One thing they did not know was that there were at least two crew members on board who had been to prison for taking the life of another. George Francis 'Paddy' McGough was an able seaman working on *Titanic* as a deck hand, virtually brushing shoulders with the passengers. In 1900 he had been convicted of manslaughter on the high seas after getting drunk and causing a fellow seaman on the collier vessel *Rustington* to fall to his death in the hold of the ship while it was moored at Santos in Brazil. Helping to fight the fire in the coal bunker was William Mintram, who had been convicted of manslaughter in 1902 after he had returned to his home in Southampton and assaulted and stabbed his own wife to death in a drunken rage.

The fire in the coal bunker was still causing problems, and John Dilley reported:

> We didn't get the fire out, and among the stokers there was talk that we would have to empty the coal bunkers after we put our passengers off in New York, and then call the fireboats there to help us put out the fire.

Wireless operators originally used the Marconi CQD distress signal. CQ was the signal to stop transmission and pay attention, and the D was added to signal distress. In 1906 the International Telegraphic Convention in Berlin created the signal SOS for summoning assistance. The letters were chosen for their simplicity in Morse code, which were three dots – three dashes – three dots. While SOS superseded CQD in 1908, Marconi operators rarely used it. Most ships at the time had only one operator, but *Titanic*, *Olympic*, *Lusitania* and *Mauretania* had two.

The wireless room had sent out about 250 messages since the journey began, and it was now very busy because the voyage was coming to an end and the passengers wanted to speak to their loved ones or make final arrangements for their arrival in New York. The procedure was for them to go to the purser's office to fill out a form that would be sent to the people manning the transmitter at Cape Race in Newfoundland. The switchboard was mounted on a raised gallery at the forward end of the generator room, which was at the back of the turbine engine room deep within the hull.

The senior operator in control of the Marconi wireless was Jack Phillips, who was experienced at his job. Jack had just celebrated his twenty-fifth birthday on the ship two days earlier, and Harold Bride* was only twenty-two, although he looked even younger than that. They alternated every six hours in manning the wireless and sleeping in a nearby bed. The wireless equipment on board was the most modern and the most powerful of any merchant ship then afloat. However, it had broken down for the whole of Saturday afternoon, probably from overuse, which caused a major problem. They managed to fix it even though they were not trained in how to do so, so they may have had help from the electricians department and Alf Allsop had been involved in the development of the new electrical switchboards. Consequently, on the Sunday there was a backlog of messages they had to catch up on.

At the same time as dealing with the backlog and the passengers, Jack and Harold were receiving messages from other ships concerning ice in the area. They had been informed by Captain Smith that icebergs were usually present more to the north of their position, but at 9 o'clock in the morning they received a message from Cunard's RMS *Coronia* stating that they had seen 'Bergs, growlers and field ice'. This was followed up at 11.40 am by a warning from SS *Noordam*, which was also on its way to New York, simply stating that they had seen 'Much ice'. At 1.42 pm RMS *Baltic* warned of 'Icebergs, and large quantities of field ice'. At 7.30 pm Harold overheard a transmission from SS *Californian* to its fellow Leyland Line ship the SS *Antillian* stating that they had seen 'Three large bergs five miles to the southward of us'.

Harold said:

> There were three rooms in the wireless cabin. One was a sleeping room, one a dynamo room, and one an operating room. I took off my clothes and went to sleep in the bed. Then I was conscious of waking up and hearing Phillips sending to Cape Race. I read what he was sending. It was only routine matter.

Violet Jessop had become friends with Jock Hume, the band's Scottish violinist, and it was a habit of hers to have a walk on deck to get some fresh air before she retired for the night. On the Saturday evening as she walked leisurely along she thought to herself 'If the sun did fail to shine so brightly on the fourth day out, and if the little nip crept into the air as evening set in, it only served to emphasize the warmth and luxuriousness within'.

The eight members of the orchestra were required to perform as two separate bands. There was a quintet with band leader Wallace Hartley* and John Hume on violin, Wesley Woodward and Percy Taylor playing the cello, and John Clarke* on base. A trio consisted of Theo Brailey* on the piano, with two non-Brits of George Krins on violin and the youngest member of the band, Roger Bricoux, playing the cello. The quintet performed at tea time and for the occasional after-dinner concerts. The trio played in the A Le Carte Restaurant and the Cafe Parisien. In all they had to learn the 350 tunes that appeared in the songbook handed out to first-class passengers.

Wallace had spent a week with his new fiancée, Maria, in Boston Spa, and having not been to see his parents before he left for America, he wrote them a letter in which he alluded to the wealth on the ship and suggested he was looking forward to receiving some good 'tips' from the passengers:

> Just a line to say that we have got away all right. It's been a bit of a rush but I am just getting a little settled. This is a fine ship and there ought to be plenty of money on her.
>
> I've missed coming home very much and it would have been nice to have seen you all if only for an hour or two, but I couldn't manage it.
>
> We have a fine band and the boys seem very nice.
>
> I have had to buy some linen and I sent my washing home today by post.
>
> I will probably arrive home on the Sunday morning. We are due here on the Saturday. I'm glad mother's foot is better.

The quintet played at the Sunday service that morning. Esther Hart had been feeling sick all Saturday and did not eat or drink, but she had got over it by Sunday morning and she and Eva attended the service. Eva sang the popular hymn *Oh Lord Our Help in Ages Past*. Esther said 'That is the hymn she sang so nicely, so she sang out loud'. Esther wrote that as a treat 'She [Eva] has had a nice ball and a box of toffee and a photo of this ship bought her today'. After lunch they met Esther's husband Ben in the library, where Esther and Eva wrote a letter intended for her mother in Chadwell Heath. The sea must have been a bit unsettled at the time as Esther pointed out 'You see the letter all of a screw is when she rolls and shakes my arm'.

There were at least twelve dogs on the ship. Most of the bigger animals were kept in kennels on F deck, while others, especially the small ones, were kept in their cabins and out of sight. Several big dogs could be seen being walked regularly along the promenades. There were several birds including four roosters and a hen belonging to Ella White of New York, and a canary. Like most ships, *Titanic* had a cat as a mascot. It was named Jenny and was also expected to help to keep the ship's population of rats and mice in order. Jenny had transferred from *Olympic*, and had recently given birth. It has been suggested that Jenny and her kittens had left the ship before she sailed, but Violet Jessop recorded that the cat lived in the galley and 'laid her family near Jim the scullion, whose approval she always sought and who always gave her warm devotion'.

It was reported that arrangements were being made to hold a dog show during the afternoon of 15 April, and in the evening a concert in aid of the Sailors' Home in Southampton was planned to take place, at which Esther and Eva intended to sing.

As the day went on the various passengers went about their business. In first class, Adolph Saalfeld apparently name-dropped to good effect:

> The name of my friend, the White Star manager in London, works wonders, and I have a small table for two to myself. I made a very good dinner and had two cigars in the smoke room and shall now go to bed as I am tired. But for a slight vibration you would not know that you are at sea.

Adolph could regularly be seen taking a number of little test tube-like glass bottles out of a black leather satchel he sometimes carried and checking them like they were the most precious things in his life. In fact, they were the reason for his trip to America. He had had the good business sense to diversify into the booming perfumery trade, and he hoped to take advantage of the expanding market in America. He had selected a collection of fragrances, which he put into the sixty-five small glass vials.

About twenty-six couples were on their way to spend their honeymoon in America. In second class, a businessman named Harry Fawnthorpe could be seen walking hand-in-hand with a young woman named Lizzie*, who he described as his new wife. However, Lizzie was actually someone else's wife.

Also in second class, a few suspicious eyes must also have noticed that Mr and Mrs Marshall did not really look suited to each other. She was a sheepish teenager with a broad Midlands accent and he was a very business-like individual with a southern accent who must have been pushing forty. She was wearing a diamond-encrusted sapphire pendant that caught everyone's eye – just the type of thing an older man might buy for a young mistress perhaps? They said they were on their way to California, hoping the climate there would help him to get over a recent illness he had suffered; which was exactly the excuse he had given his family – including his wife and daughter.

In truth, his name was Henry Samuel Morley, a senior partner in his family's confectionary business in Worcester. Kate Florence Phillips* was an employee who worked in one of his sweet shops, and they had begun a secret affair that had developed in such a way that Henry was prepared to abandon his family and take Kate to resettle on the west coast of America. Once they had made up their minds to act upon their feelings, Henry sold two of his shops and gave all the money to his wife and daughter for their security. Although the people around them must have had their suspicions, it is said that the only other person who knew about the affair was Henry's brother, who had actually agreed to drive them to Southampton, and is said to have waved them off.

Joseph Fynney* was in his mid-thirties, and was described as a 'handsome bachelor' with 'black hair, a smooth face, being a height of 5 feet 6 inches tall'. He often travelled to Montreal to visit his family, and it is likely that some of the crew who worked on various ships had noticed how strange it was that each time he made the trip he had a young male companion with him. On this occasion it was an eighteen-year-old lad called Alfred Gaskell, who lived close to the church in Liverpool where Joe worked with delinquents. They shared a cabin on the same second-class ticket, and some passengers must have thought their situation was quite unusual to say the least; there were probably many frowning looks and gossiping tongues.

Talking with a slight French accent, Louis Hoffman* led other passengers to believe that he was a widower, but they noticed that he was reluctant to get into conversation with anyone, especially concerning his two boys, Lolo and Momon. He was very protective of them and never let them out of his sight. A French-speaking Swiss woman named Bertha Lehmann had stayed in her cabin every day suffering from seasickness, but after a few days she started to get used to the situation, and on feeling a little better she went up to the dining room to try to eat something. Louis and the boys were sat at the same table, and for some reason he felt he could trust her, and on being asked if he would like a game of cards, he asked Bertha to watch them for a while so he could.

Two young men with Welsh accents from third class named Dai Bowen* and Leslie Williams* were seen to go off training each day. They were considered to be highly promising boxers who were on their way to the United States for a series of boxing contests. A South Wales newspaper noted:

> Mr Torreyson, a well-known Pittsburgh racing man, wrote to a Cardiff newspaper reporter named Charles A Barnett, offering to defray the expenses of two good Welsh boxers. Many applications were received, and Williams and Bowen were selected as men likely to meet with success. Bowen was a featherweight of considerable promise. In the contests he had fought in he showed signs of developing into a splendid man. Williams, a bantamweight, was the more experienced boxer.

It was recorded by Charles Barnett:

> It seems but a moment ago since the two young boxers gripped my hand in farewell from the train which took them to Southampton. What strange fate! They were definitely fixed-up to sail by the Lusitania four days earlier, but poor Leslie Williams called on me to say that he wanted to wait for some suits of clothes to be made, as things were rather dear in America.
>
> 'Very well!' I said, 'we will go to the shipping agent and see what other boats are going, and I will send another cable to say that you are not going by the *Lusitania*'.
>
> We immediately went to the agent's office, and when Leslie heard that the world's largest liner was going to make a maiden trip on the following Wednesday he was simply delighted.
>
> 'That will give me a few days over the holidays' he remarked to the manager of the office, and then left for home.

They were considering themselves to be very fortunate indeed. Three other boxers had been chosen to go to the States at first, but because of other commitments they could not make the trip, so Dai and Leslie were asked to go instead. A newspaper reported:

> Fred Dyer was next approached, and would have accepted, for, as he stated: 'his luck had been so bad over here in the way of accidents and interruptions to matches which had been arranged that he felt it could not be any worse in America and might be better.
>
> But just before going down to Nazareth House he saw another specialist about his knee, and was strongly advised to rest it absolutely for the next three months.

To top it all, Mr Torreyson had also paid a little extra for their tickets so that they could have use of the first-class passengers' gymnasium.

Still known to his mother as David John and not Dai, he had written a letter to her and posted it in Queenstown:

> I am just writing you a few lines before I go sick, for I have been very good so far. This is a lovely boat, she is very near as big as Treherbert, she is like a floating palace, if you walk from one end of her to the other you are tired. We are landing in France the time I am writing you this, you don't know whether she is moving or not for she goes very steady. Dear Mother, I hope that you won't worry yourself about me, I can tell you that I am a lot better than I thought I would be, for we gets plenty of fun on board. We met two Swansea boys at the station, so you see that I get plenty of company. There are hundreds of foreigners on her of every nation. The food we get here is very good but not as good as dear old home. We have no boxing gloves with us; they would be no good if we did have some. Remember me to Martha Jane and Jack and Tommy Ostler. Tell Morris and Stephen that if I will feel like I do now when I land in Yankee Land I shall be alright. I shan't give you an address now, not until I land for it won't be worth it. I did not see David Rees in Southampton at all. Remember me to all I know, tell Stephen to tell all the boys that I am enjoying myself alright so far. If James tell you that I have not

> wrote to him, tell him that I can't do it very good now, you can show him this if you like, for it will be the same I shall have to say now for the time being as I am telling you. I hope you will excuse the pencil for I have no pen and ink, so cheer up now mother, for I am in the pink, so don't vex. I think I will draw to a close now in wishing you all my best love.

Other noted sportsmen on the ship included tennis player Karl Howell Baer. In 1907 he had played in the United States Davis Cup squad, and was the Wimbledon doubles runner-up. Richard Norris Williams was also making his name in the sport of tennis. He was travelling with his father, and was on his way to try to enhance his career playing in tennis tournaments before going on to Harvard University.

Charles Eugene Williams was a successful racquets player. He had won the English Open title in 1911, and the World Championship early in 1912; he was on his way to defend his title in New York.

John Borie Ryerson was a promising young golfer, who, like Dick Williams had a successful career in front of him.

James Clinch Smith was a member of most of New York's elite clubs. He was a skilful yachtsman, and a multi-prize-winning rider at the New York Horse Show. He had actually built his own track at Smithtown.

William Ernest Carter was travelling with his socialite wife, Lucille, their two daughters and a nephew. William was a good horseman and a keen polo player, and they had been staying at Melton Mowbray in Leicestershire, where he managed a few games of his favourite sport and also found time to go hunting with the local foxhounds.

Washington Augustus Roebling was a veteran of the battle of Gettysburg in 1863, and he had supervised the building of the Brooklyn Bridge in New York, opened in 1883. He had been a promising American football player in his youth, but his fascination with motor cars prompted him to join the pioneers of the early days of motor sport. He designed and built his own car, the Roebling-Planche Racer, in which he finished second in the Vanderbilt Cup in 1911. He was returning from a motoring tour of Europe.

Tommie Andrews was a keen cricketer, and all the Andrews men played for the North Down Cricket Club in Comber. They even donated the ground that is still used by the club to this day, and a trophy for the player of the year. He organised a game between North Down CC and Harland and Wolff CC, and he chose to play for his works team, but the North Down bowlers got him out without scoring.

Chief Engineer Peter Sloan was a member of the Valkyrie Football Club in Liverpool, and during his employment with a number of the White Star ships in the Western and Mediterranean trades he won the half-mile championship for swimming during the Italy versus England gala at Spezia, and the gold medal and silver cup.

His second-in-command was a Mancunian named Alfred Allsop*, who had become fascinated with the power of electricity when he was still a young lad. He was often seen at the Salford power station, or riding on the electric tram cars in Manchester, eager to know how they worked and how they were powered. It is said that Fred had secured a place as a cabin attendant on *Titanic* for his friend, George Lionel Payne, but George was fortunate enough to miss the boat-train connection from Manchester owing to fog.

In addition to Adolph Saalfeld, two other Jewish passengers were Abraham Harmer* and Joseph Hyman*. Abraham was in his mid-20s and seemed to be very cagey or hesitant when anyone asked his name. It is likely that some of the stewards wondered why he didn't always answer them right away when they called him Mr Harmer from somewhere not directly in his view. That was because he was actually a Latvian jeweller called David Livshin. He had swapped his ticket with another man and had decided to travel in the other man's name so as not to cause any confusion. He had left his pregnant wife back at their home in Salford, and was travelling to visit his sisters in Montreal, where he intended to set up a new life and send for his wife after she had their baby. Joseph was also on his way to prepare a new life for his family in America.

Marian Meanwell clutched her black crocodile skin handbag, as she chatted with fellow third-class passengers, telling them that her beloved daughter Margaret had gone to America in search of adventure. She happily told others that her daughter was a very talented ballet dancer, and the audiences simply loved her performances. In fact, Margaret had married an acrobat and had found employment working with a circus in New York City. Marian had crossed the Atlantic a number of times to visit her, but Margaret had become widowed in April 1911, when her husband had died of consumption, and she was left with two young children, aged six and two, to look after. When she was given the prospect of returning to work, Marian had offered to move to New York and look after the children.

George Dunton Widener, a Philadelphia banker, held a dinner party in the à la carte restaurant in honour of Captain Smith. At about nine o'clock the captain excused himself and went to the bridge. After the ladies retired, the men sat in the first-class smoking room in conversation. They were still there when the ship struck the iceberg.

Arthur Gee and Adolphe Saalfeld dined in the Cafe Parisien as they listened to the trio play their light music. Afterwards they also retired to the first class smoking room, where Arthur joined two other businessmen; an American named Charles Jones, and Algernon Barkworth*. Adolph settled down in a chair to relax. 'Algie' was of an old Yorkshire family on his way to spend a month or so in Massachusetts. He stated 'Coming over I made the acquaintance of two most agreeable chaps …'

Tom Whiteley noted:

> It was the gayest night of the trip (14 April) among the diners. We had made great time, and the probability was the trip would be a record-breaker. Orders had been issued Sunday to make the dinner the finest ever served on a ship, regardless of expense, and the orders were carried out … The one topic of conversation was the new boat and the speed she was making … At one time Doctor O'Loughlin stood up, and, raising a glass of champagne, cried, 'Let us drink to the mighty *Titanic*'. With cries of approval, everybody drank to the toast. I believe it was generally thought by all of those at the tables that *Titanic* would reach New York late Tuesday or early Wednesday morning, and the captain and other officers were planning a big banquet after the landing in anticipation of the trip record breaker. The dinner broke up shortly before 9 o'clock, and the men retired to the smoking rooms, while some of the women went to their staterooms, and others strolled along the promenade. We cleared the dining-room about 10 o'clock and soon after I went to bed.

Second Officer Charles Lightoller* came on watch duty at six o'clock in the evening. Before nine o'clock both he and Captain Smith had remarked on how quickly the temperature was dropping, yet the weather was clear and the sea unusually calm. It was a starlit night, which Charles believed would reflect light off any icebergs that might be nearby. At 9.20 pm Captain Smith, in reference to some iceberg warnings they had received, left Charles with the instructions: 'If in the slightest degree doubtful, let me know.'

At half past nine Charles instructed Sixth Officer Jim Moody to telephone the crow's nest and ask the men there to keep a sharp lookout for small ice and to pass the word to subsequent watches. He was relieved by First Officer Murdoch at ten o'clock. He did his rounds, covering the decks and hundreds of feet of ladders and staircases, and retired to his cabin.

At 9:40 pm, while Harold Bride was asleep in his bunk intending to relieve his flustered colleague at midnight, Jack received the most serious message to date, which came from another Leyland ship, the MV *Mesaba* stating 'Saw much pack ice and great numbers of large icebergs; also field ice. Weather good, clear.' The co-ordinates suggested that the ice field was right in path of *Titanic*.

However, at the same time numerous passengers had just finished their dinner and, as the boat was making good speed they thought it was possible that they would arrive in New York later on the following day, so they wanted to send their last messages. Consequently, Jack was being swamped by people waving their purser authority notes at him and he was exceptionally busy. He interrupted the *Mesaba* operator by replying with the words: 'Keep out! Shut up! You're jamming my signal. I'm working Cape Race!' Because he was so preoccupied with the passengers, he did not send the message to the bridge, and the message should have been sent with the prefix MSG – 'Masters Service Gram' which meant that the captain was obliged to acknowledge receipt of it. Later he told Officer Lightoller 'I just put the message under a paperweight at my elbow, just until I squared up what I was doing before sending it to the Bridge'.

The final ice warning message was received at 10.30 pm from SS *Californian* stating 'We are stopped and surrounded by ice'. However, although it was obvious that *Titanic* was approaching a minefield of dangerous waters, this message was also not sent to the bridge.

4. 'Iceberg Ahead!'

Each watch up in the crow's nest is four hours long. Fred Fleet* and Reg Lee took over the watch at 10 pm, and Archie Jewell passed on to them the information from the bridge as he had been told to do.

Reg Lee reported later 'There was a good deal of haze ahead. It thickened, but the speed of the vessel was not slackened.' Just after seven bells (11.30 pm), Fred saw a black mass ahead, immediately struck three straight bells and telephoned the bridge.

The use of bells to tell the time comes from the time when sailors could not afford a personal timepiece. Three straight bells were used in an emergency, whereas 3AM was marked by two bells followed by a pause before the third. He reported 'Iceberg right ahead.' While he was still on the telephone the ship started veering to the left (portside). However, as Fred and Reg continued to look with bated breath, they were alarmed when the crow's nest began to shake as they saw the right side of the ship (starboard) scrape alongside the iceberg, and the collision caused ice to fall on the decks. They had hoped that the bridge had taken action in time and that it had been a near miss with no severe damage done, so they remained in the crow's nest until being relieved at midnight, about twenty minutes later.

Reg Lee reported what he saw: 'The iceberg appeared to be a dark mass, and the only white spot on it was a fringe along the top. It was first seen at about half-a-mile or less distant.'

Joe Scarrott stated:

> It was a beautiful starlight night, no wind, and the sea was as calm as a lake, but the air was very cold. Everybody was in good spirits and everything throughout the ship was going smoothly.
>
> All of a sudden she crashed into an iceberg, which shook the giant liner from stem to stern. The shock of the collision was not so great as one would expect considering the size of the iceberg and the speed the ship was going, which was about 22 knots an hour. I was underneath the forecastle enjoying a smoke at the time. It happened about twenty minutes to twelve o'clock. The shaking of

> the ship seemed as though the engines had suddenly been reversed to full speed astern. Those of the crew who were asleep in their bunks turned out, and we all rushed on deck to see what was the matter.
>
> We found there was a large quantity of ice and snow on the starboard side of the fore deck. We did not think it very serious so we went below again cursing the iceberg for disturbing us. We had no sooner got below when the boatswain called all hands on deck to uncover and turn all the boats out ready for lowering. We did not think then there was anything serious. The general idea of the crew was that we were going to get the boats ready in case of emergency, and the sooner we got the job done the quicker we should get below again.'

John Dilley was busy with his back-aching work when the ship struck the iceberg:

> It was right under bunker 6 that the iceberg tore the biggest hole, and the flood that came through *Titanic* put out the fire that our tons of water hadn't been able to get rid of.
>
> The stokers were beginning to get alarmed over it, but the officers told us to keep our mouths shut. They didn't want to alarm the passengers. Another fireman said that because of the fire the ship sank more rapidly than otherwise would have been the case.

It had been necessary to take the coal out of sections two and three on the starboard side forward, and when the water came rushing in after the collision the bulkheads would not hold because they did not have the supporting weight of the coal.

Somebody reported to Chief Engineer Joe Bell that the forward bulkhead had given way and he replied 'My God, we are lost'.

Fred Barrett was working in the number six boiler room of stokehole ten, where there were eight firemen and four trimmers on duty and a young Lancastrian named Jonathan Shepherd* was the engineer. Fred recalled:

> There is a clock face in the stokehole and a red light goes up for 'Stop'. I was talking to Harry Hesketh when the red light came

up, and having to make a quick decision, I shouted, 'Shut all the dampers'. That order was obeyed, but the crash came before we had them all shut.

There was a rush of water into my stokehole. Harry and I were standing on plates about six feet above the tank tops, and the water came in about two feet above the plates. The water-tight door between the sections was then open, and we jumped through the doorway into boiler room 5, the door of which dropped down and closed just as we got to the other side. The door is worked from the Bridge, and I was unaware if any more men in my stokehole were saved. The only one I saw afterwards was George Beauchamp. We saw that the damage extended into boiler room 5, and water was coming in fast enough through the side of the ship to flood the place.

Shortly afterwards the order came from the engine room to send all the stokers up, and most of them went, but I was told to remain with the engineers to do any errands, so I, along with Bert Harvey, Bertie Wilson and Jonathan Shepherd waited in boiler room 5. The lights suddenly went out and Bert told me to send some firemen for some lamps, and just as they got the lamps the electric light came on again. They must have been changing the dynamos over. Bert then told me to fetch some firemen to draw the furnaces, so I climbed up the emergency ladder, and seeing two firemen on what was called Scotland Road, I ordered them to get some other firemen and about 15 men took about 20 minutes to draw the 30 furnaces in the section. On completing the task, I told them to go back up to the top, and on looking at the gauge I saw that there was no water in the boilers. The ship had emptied them while blowing off steam.

Bert told me to lift a manhole plate to gain access to some valves, which I did, and then Mr Shepherd, hurrying across the steam-filled room to do something and not noticing the plate had been removed, fell down and broke his leg. They lifted him up and laid him in the pump-room. As they attended to him, about a quarter of an hour after the fires were drawn there was a rush of water as the bulkhead separating sections 5 and 6 gave way. Bert ordered me to get up top and I left the two men to their fate.

Chief Stewardess Sarah Stap*, the daughter of a master mariner, was responsible for Mrs Astor and Lady Gordon Duff Grant:

> I was in bed and was awakened by the slight bump. It would then have been about a quarter to twelve at night. I did not take very much heed of the noise at first, because I had been used to ships bumping before. In fact I thought that something or other had gone wrong in the engine room.
>
> Presently, I heard the night watch-man pass my door and I called out to him, 'What's the matter?' He replied, 'Oh, we have only touched a bit of ice. I think it is alright. I don't think it is anything.'
>
> It was three quarters of an hour after I felt the ship bump that I got up, and when I reached the deck the lifeboats had been ordered out. I was not in the least frightened. I was simply stunned.
>
> Perfect order prevailed and everybody seemed calm and collected. The passengers would not believe that we had struck an iceberg, but I myself knew what had happened. The officers and crew behaved magnificently, as did also the dear old captain.

Tom Threlfall*, a fireman from Liverpool, was an experienced seaman, and he stated how:

> My watch went down to our duty in the stokeholds after the ship had struck, and on an order from the Bridge we were sent up on deck at 1.20 am by the engineers, who themselves stayed to die at their posts. Mr Lowe, the fifth officer, 'a gentleman and a Britisher', kept the boats of survivors together under his command.
>
> My watch was asleep when we were awakened by a shout 'Get up; we've run into something'. I got up and saw the tarpaulin over a hatch bulging out with the pressure of water underneath. The water was pouring down the passage from our room into the stokehold. The ship had torn herself right open from Number 6 section to the fore-hatch. We waded along the passage with our clothes to the mess deck. Then the boatswain piped 'all hands,' and the second engineer told me to take my watch below. We went down to the stokehold to draw the fires. At about 1.20 am Mr Hesketh, the second engineer, said, 'We've done all we can men. Get out now.'

Caroline Bonnell spoke of how she and her cousin had been looking forward to seeing at least one iceberg during the voyage:

> 'Well, thank goodness, Nathalie, we are going to see our iceberg at last.' That simple, foolish little sentence was the one thing of all others that I said to my cousin as the great, beautiful *Titanic* was shivering beneath her blow.
>
> Nathalie Wick and I were lying in our berths half asleep when the blow came. It was terrible. For a second the whole boat just stood stock still in its swift tracks, and then it gave a great shiver all through. When we got out onto the deck everything was as calm as an August afternoon. The sea was as smooth as glass. There wasn't a berg or an ice floe in sight, and the sky was just thick with stars. I never saw so many stars in my life as there were that night. The water glittered blue with their glow.
>
> We had just decided to go back to bed when an officer about came up to us and to another group of people who had gotten up to find out what was the matter.
>
> 'Go below, and put on your lifebelts,' he said, 'you may need them later.'
>
> We went down at once and told my aunt and uncle, Mr and Mrs George Wick, what we had been told. Uncle George just laughed at us.
>
> 'Why, that's nonsense girls', he said. 'This boat is all right. She's going along nicely. She just got a glancing blow, I guess.'
>
> That's the way everyone seemed to thing, and we went into out stateroom, but in a minute or so an officer knocked at the door and told us to go up on the A Deck. He said that there was really no danger and it was just a precautionary measure.

Clear Cameron* and Nellie Wallcroft had retired to bed at about half past ten and they were asleep when the collision occurred. Nellie had heard a crash and was nearly thrown from her berth. She woke Clear up and said 'Clear, what's that?'. They noticed that engines had stopped, but they stayed in their cabin till a steward arrived and said "Go back to your beds, there is no danger!" However, someone outside shouted "an iceberg".

Joseph Hyman had been in bed for over two hours when he felt the jolt:

My stateroom was in the third class cabin, well forward, and about two decks down from the top deck. Sunday night I sat chatting with several other passengers and went to bed a few minutes after ten o'clock. It must have been about half-past-eleven when I was awakened by a terrible shock. There was only one – just a bang and a rip – lasting a couple of seconds. Then everything was quiet. I didn't know what had happened, but never dreamed it could be anything serious, so lay in my bunk for twenty minutes listening. I could hear doors banging and passengers running to and fro asking what was the matter. Someone said everything was all right, but some were afraid.

Then I got up and dressed and went out into the passage. A steward standing there told me roughly to go to the back of the ship, and I walked along the passage which ran the whole length of the vessel. On the way I passed a group of engineers and stokers, laughing, chatting and smoking cigarettes. I reached the after third class cabin, then climbed up to the top deck, where I stood fully twenty minutes. I knew the ship had hit something, but I didn't think it could be anything serious – I don't believe anybody on board suspected anything serious.

Alice Phillips* was travelling with her father. She had been frightened by the thud of the collision and was suspicious that the crew were not telling the passengers the full seriousness of the situation:

I had gone to bed on the Sunday night, but was not asleep. About a quarter to-twelve we felt an awful crash – when the boat struck an iceberg – and was nearly rocked out of bed. Soon after I heard the engines stop.

Naturally I was dreadfully frightened, and at once ran outside. Just beyond the doorway I met the cabin steward and asked him what had happened?

'Everything is all right,' he said, and advised me to go back to the cabin.

I could not understand it, and felt that there must be something amiss, but I listened to his advice, and, with many doubts, went back to the cabin.

> I rung up the steward to enquire what had happened, and he said it was nothing serious, and that we could go to sleep. I did not feel satisfied. Father came to my cabin, and asked if I would care to go on deck with him; so I did. We had not been there long when someone said 'All on deck with lifebelts on!'.

Algernon Barkworth had stayed in the smoking room:

> I was discussing in the smoking room with them (Jones and Gee) late on Sunday night the science of good road building in which I am keenly interested.
>
> I was sitting in the smoking room with my friends when we heard a grinding sound which caused the ship to tremble and the engines seemed to stop. Walking out on deck, through the smoking rooms veranda, deck A, the first person I saw was Mr T Stead and I asked him what he had seen. He said, 'an iceberg had ground against the starboard side'. I went forward and noticed the forecastle filled with pieces of ice which had fallen from the friction of the ship against the iceberg. The forecastle made a heavy list to the starboard.

Adolphe Saalfeld went down to his cabin to collect a few things, but was advised by a steward to go to the lifeboat deck. Among the items he left behind was his samples of bottled perfumes, but he had a menu card from the cafe in his pocket.

Charles Lightoller was just nodding off to sleep at about twenty minutes to midnight when he felt a grinding vibration. He went on deck in his pyjamas, where he met Third Officer Herbert Pitman who had also been disturbed by the vibration. They concluded that the vessel had hit something, but there was no sign of undue alarm on the bridge so they returned to their cabins to await orders. Ten minutes later, Fourth Officer Joe Boxhall entered his cabin and informed him that, 'The water is up to the F deck in the Mail Room'. Charles put on a pair of trousers, a pullover and a bridge coat over his pyjamas and went back out on deck.

Charles Andrews* stated:

> I came off watch about a quarter to 11 and went down and turned in. About 20 minutes after that I was woken? up by a movement of the

ship. Several of the boys woke up with the shock also. So with that I got out of my bunk and went into the working alleyway, seeing lots of stewards out. I walked up and down the alleyway several times with another steward. After that I went back to the quarters. I went back and lay down for a few minutes and then got up again. I had no sooner gotten there than somebody came and said, 'All hands on deck'.

Upon settling down in her bunk, Violet Jessop found the prayer she had with her and read it. Then she made her roommate read it too. Soon afterwards Violet was 'comfortably drowsy' but not quite asleep when the collision happened.

Kate Gold* was fast asleep:

> When the alarm, or first idea of an alarm, came to us we were sleeping. We received the notification with much amusement, and quite ignored what we thought was a joke. We were advised to get up and put our life-belts on, but we did not stir. It was only when Thomas Andrews, one of the principals of Harland and Wolff, the builders of the ship, came to us and told us to hurry up on deck that we began to realise the urgency of the situation.
>
> The ladies put on their own belts, yet were laughing and joking all the time, considering they were obeying orders which were part of a drill. When ordered to the boats, though, they began to realise otherwise.

Tom Whiteley stated:

> My quarters were on E deck, which is five decks down. I was awakened about 11:30pm. I did not feel any shock, but a shipmate of mine took me by the shoulder and said to get out. I said: 'is it 5:30am already?' He said: 'No; we've hit a berg'. I looked out of the porthole, the sea was like glass and I did not believe him. I looked on deck and found it covered with ice. Stoke hole number two began to fill with water at once. All the watertight doors were closed. They had to be opened again to let men go down and draw the fires to prevent an explosion. One fellow, I don't know who it was, went down with about twenty others and drew all the fires.

Lancastrian James Witter* stated:

> Well, I didn't think she'd hit anything, I thought she dropped a blade from the propeller you know.
>
> Well, I went down to the working out way where my cabin is, number seven glory-hole. I was standing there talking to two or three fellows and the carpenter came along and I heard him say the bloody mail room was full of water. I said, 'What's that? Mail room full of water?'. He said 'Yes'. I said, 'Well, what about those bulk-head doors forward?'. He said, 'They're not holding, Jim'.
>
> Of course then I walked into my cabin … and I opened my box. I called everybody. I said, 'Come along fellas get up, she's going down. So they opened my box, took up some matches and some cigarettes, and I said, 'Come on fellas, get out!'. 'What the hell are you talking about?' they said, 'get out of here'. Someone threw a boot at me. I said, 'Goodnight gentlemen'. Just as easy as that.

Harold Bride was concerned for his workmate and didn't really sense any alarm:

> I remember how tired he (Phillips) was and got out of bed to relieve him. I didn't even feel the shock. I hardly knew it had happened until after the captain had come to us. There was no jolt whatsoever. I was standing by Phillips telling him to go to bed when the captain put his head into the cabin.
>
> 'We've struck an iceberg,' the captain said, 'and I'm having an inspection made to tell what it has done for us. You better get ready to send out a call for assistance. But don't send it until I tell you'.
>
> The captain went away, and in ten minutes, I should estimate the time, he came back. We could hear a terrible confusion outside, but there was not the least thing to indicate that there was any trouble. The wireless was working perfectly.
>
> 'Send the call for assistance,' said the captain, barely putting his head in the door.
>
> 'What call should I send?' asked Phillips.
>
> 'The regulation international call for help, just that.' Then the captain was gone.

Phillips began to send 'C Q D' – he flashed away at it and we were joking while he did so. All of us made light of the disaster. We joked that way while he flashed signals for about five minutes. Then the captain came back.

'What are you sending?' he asked.

'C Q D,' Phillips replied.

The humour of the situation appealed to me. I cut in with a little remark that made us all laugh, including the captain.

'Send S O S,' I said, 'It's the new call, and it may be your last chance to send it'.

Phillips, with a laugh, changed the signal to 'S O S'.

The captain told us we had been struck amidships, or just aft of amidships. It was ten minutes, Phillips told me, after he noticed the iceberg, but the slight jolt was the only signal to us that a collision had occurred. We thought we were a good distance away. We said lots of funny things to each other in the next few minutes. We picked up the first steamship *Frankfurt*; gave her our position and said we had struck an iceberg and needed assistance.

The *Frankfurt* operator went away to tell his captain. He came back, and we told him we were sinking by the head, and that we could observe a distinct list forward.

The *Carpathia* answered our signal, and we told her our position, and said we are sinking by the head. The operator went to tell the captain, and in five minutes returned, and told us the *Carpathia* was putting about and heading for us.

Our captain had left us at this time, and Phillips told me to run and tell him what the *Carpathia* had answered. I did so, and I went through an awful mass of people to his cabin (the wheelhouse). The decks were full of scrambling men and women.

I came back and heard Phillips giving the *Carpathia* further directions. Phillips told me to put on my clothes. Until that moment I forgot I wasn't dressed. I went to my cabin and dressed. I brought an overcoat to Phillips, and as it was very cold I slipped the overcoat upon him while he worked.

Every few minutes Phillips would send me to the captain with little messages. They were merely telling how *Carpathia* was coming our way, and giving her speed.

5. 'All Hands on Deck!'

Word began to get around that the ship had hit an iceberg, so a lot of the passengers went to the front of the ship to see.

Algernon Barkworth was one of these and he stated 'I was found by several friends and went up to the boat deck and heard the order given to put on our lifebelts. We returned to our cabins and put them on and went up again on deck.'

Caroline Bonnell noted:

> When we got on the deck uncle and aunt were there, and I went down again to another part of the steamer and got my Aunt Elizabeth. When I got back with her, there were crowds of people standing all around. Nobody seemed very excited; everyone was talking, and it seemed to be the general idea that we would soon be ordered back to bed. Just then an officer came up to us and said we should go up to the next deck – the boat deck!
>
> By that time everyone was up. Mrs John Jacob Astor was there, sitting in a steamer chair. Her husband, Colonel Astor, was beside her, and her maid was helping her to finish her dressing. There was no confusion here even yet, though we noticed that the boat was beginning to list to starboard.

Clear Cameron and Nellie dressed and went on deck, and they were walking around trying to find out more information on the situation when the distress flares went up. The orders were to load the boats beginning at the front on the port side, working back, and then back forward on the starboard side, and they finally entered lifeboat 14 as the ship was listing badly, less than an hour before it sank. Officer Harold Lowe was in command. He fired his pistol twice over the side of the ship, to keep men away from the lifeboat. Then it was lowered and they rowed away.

Joseph Hyman stated:

All around me were passengers putting on life belts. Some of the women were a little frightened, but most were calm, and I thought the life belts were just an extra precaution. I looked for one but couldn't find one. There were several back in my room, but I never thought to bring one along. I saw several people climbing up the stairs which led to a sort of house on the deck just in front of me, and I thought I would see what was the matter up there. I asked several officers if there was any danger, and they said 'No, no; just keep calm'.

I climbed up the stairs, and there were a lot of men and women standing about a lifeboat. The women were being helped in, but the men didn't seem to want to get in. Then I noticed that it was the next to the last boat in that part of the ship. The others were all lowered, and I got a little uneasy. I climbed up onto the rail, and watching my chance, slipped into the boat just before they began to lower away. Most of the men thought they would be safer back on the boat, and some of them smiled at us as we went down.

In a letter to her family, Alice Phillips stated:

I heard shouts and the sounds of general confusion on the deck, and determined to at least see what was being done for myself. Without a moment's further hesitation I rushed to the upper deck, and no sooner had I got there than someone picked me up and put me into one of the lifeboats (number 12).

I cannot tell you, dear, how I felt in that moment. Dad and I got our belts on, and I went on deck again, and then all the women and children were put into lifeboats and lowered. I saw my dear father for the last time in this world, and I almost felt I would have liked to die with him.

There were already a large number of other women and children in the boat, and I had not been in it a few moments, and did not even fully understand what was the matter, when it was pushed off into darkness. That was the last I saw of *Titanic*, and I shall never see my poor father again.

Lizzie Wilkinson remembered:

> I was asleep at the time of the collision, but awakened by the shock. When I rushed upon the deck I was ordered into a lifeboat, but I feared to trust myself in one of the frail craft. While officers with drawn revolvers issued their orders, one of the men forced me bodily into the second boat …

Fireman Threlfall noted that 'Every survivor agrees that no one on board realised the danger of the ship's condition. "Just go for a spin round" was the phrase often used to persuade women to get into the boats'.

As soon as the officers realised that the situation was serious, Charles Lightoller took charge of the even number lifeboats on the port side, but owing to the noise of the ship's exhausts letting off steam it was difficult for anyone to be heard and he had to use hand signals to convey messages. As soon as he received the orders, he began to try loading women and children into lifeboat 4, but the windows on A-Deck were locked, so he switched to loading lifeboat 6. Henry Wilde was cautious about allowing the boats to be lowered, but Charles, having had experience of a previous shipwreck, got permission from the captain to lower the boats. He managed to persuade about 25 people to get into lifeboat 6 and started lowering it. As the boat descended he realised that there was only one seaman in the boat. Charles called for a seaman, and Major Arthur Peuchen, an experienced yachtsman, volunteered. He was the only male passenger Charles allowed into a lifeboat that night. Lifeboats 8, 12, 14 and 16 were got away at regular intervals before half past one.

Around this time he took Henry Wilde, Captain Smith and William Murdock to the first officer's cabin, where they armed themselves. On his return to the deck he helped to load lifeboat 4. He tried to remove a thirteen-year-old boy from the boat, but was persuaded by the boy's father to allow him to stay. Just then a group of men took over lifeboat 2, and Charles regained control by threatening them with an empty gun. The lifeboat and passengers was lowered at five minutes to two.

Then the collapsible D dinghy was lifted and hooked to the tackles where lifeboat 2 had been. The crew then formed a ring around the craft and allowed only women to pass through. The boat could hold 47, but only 15 women stepped on board, so Charles allowed men to take the vacant seats. Then Colonel Gracie arrived with more female passengers and all the men immediately stepped out and made way for them. Henry Wilde asked Charles to go with the lifeboat, but Charles retorted 'Not damn likely,' and he stepped back on deck. While the collapsible was lowered to the ocean, two men were seen to jump into it from the rapidly flooding A deck.

Charles still had collapsible A and B to get off. As the water rose on the boat deck, he climbed on to the top of the officer's quarters and stripped the covers and cut away the ropes with a penknife. He was able to send it down to the flooded deck. Just then *Titanic* took a great plunge forward. He turned to face the sea and dived in. He had started to swim clear when he was sucked against the grating of one of the large ventilator shafts, and he was taken down with the ship. As the water hit the still hot boilers, the blast blew him back to the surface, where he found himself alongside the capsized collapsible B. As *Titanic* went under, the forward funnel broke loose and toppled his way, narrowly missing him.

Charles Andrews:

> walked up on deck and stood by my boat. There were lots of people around, and I saw stores brought to the boat, and bread. I did not see the stores put in the boat. I assisted in helping the ladies and children into the boat. After the boat was full the officer called out for able seamen, or any individuals then, to man the boat.

Walter Lord's *A Night to Remember* stated:

> Chief Baker Charles Joughin has just spent some time and energy around 1:45am tossing chairs out into the ocean in an attempt to give swimmers something to hold on to. It was tiring work; so after he lugged the last chair to the edge and squeezed it thru the window (it was like threading a needle) Joughin retired to the pantry on the starboard side of A Deck. It was 2:10. As he quenched his thirst, this time it was water (he was up to that point getting, well, drunk) he heard a crash as thought something had buckled.
>
> He kept out of the crush as much as possible and ran along the rear of the crowd. He vaulted over the steps to B Deck, then to the well deck. Just as he got there, Titanic gave a sickening twist to port, throwing people into a huge heap along the port rail. Only

> Joughin kept his balance. He slipped over the starboard rail and stood on the actual side of the ship. He worked his way up the side still holding onto the rail from the outside. Anyway, he rides down the stern like Jack-n-Rose and just bloops off the boat without getting his hair wet! And then, because of his heft and all the alcohol, he was OK to just dog paddle around until the *Carpathia* came hours later!
>
> He gave this statement at the British enquiry: 'I got to the starboard side of the poop; found myself in the water. I do not believe my head went under at all. I thought I saw some wreckage, swam towards it and found collapsible boat (B) with Lightoller and about twenty-five men on it. There was no room for me. I tried to get on, but was pushed off, but I hung around. I got around to the opposite side and cook Maynard, who recognised me, helped me and held on to me.

Harry Eches was off duty when the collision occurred, and on hearing some commotion he became curious and walked down E Deck and along the alleyway known as Scotland Road. As he entered the third-class accommodation he came upon a passenger carrying a lump of ice who must have tried in vain to get others to believe that the ship had hit an iceberg and was in danger. He dropped the ice to the floor and exclaimed 'Will you believe me now?'. Harry took the hint and went along the corridors trying to stir the passengers into action. He banged on the door of cabin C-78, and when the people inside asked what the trouble was Harry explained, but despite his warnings the occupants did not open the door, so he moved on.

On returning to his station he spent his time trying to get the first-class passengers to put on their lifebelts. Ben Guggenheim protested, saying 'This will hurt!' and only agreed to wear his after a great deal of persuasion. Harry gave the tycoon a thick sweater to wear before leading him out onto the boat deck. However, Mr Guggenheim soon returned to his cabin to put on his best velvet evening wear, and his friends did the same. He later stated to fellow passengers 'We've dressed up in our best and are prepared to go down like gentlemen'.

One of Jack Butterworth's colleagues left an account stating:

> A number of my fellow stewards were not conscious of the accident, and they had to be aroused from their sleep. We had great

difficulty in calling Butterworth, and when we got him out of his berth he said, in a sleepy voice: 'What's up?'. He was not saved.

Tom Whiteley remembered:

The order came: 'All hands above decks with lifebelts!' The deck was crowded. The second officer was getting lifeboat 1 ready. He asked me to give him a hand. I helped fill the boats. They were crowded with women and children. There were two collapsible boats on each side in addition to the regular lifeboats. At the order of the second officer we got the collapsible boat on the port side ready and lifeboat 1 on the starboard followed. The collapsible lifeboat 2 on the starboard jammed. I got my leg caught in one of the ropes. The second officer was hacking at the rope with a knife. I was being dragged around the deck by that rope, when I looked up and saw the boat filled with people turning end up on the davits. The boat overturned.

There was a bit of a panic when it first happened. The officers had to use their revolvers. The chief officer shot one man – I didn't see this, but three others did – and then he shot himself. But everybody behaved splendidly, especially the firemen. It was a black berg we struck, and though the night was clear it was impossible to see one of that colour. I saw another like it when drifting on that overturned lifeboat. The berg Titanic hit was on the starboard bow, and they were doing twenty-five knots, trying to break the record to New York.

William Wynn stated:

I went up on the fore-well deck and asked what was the matter. I saw a lot of men passengers there, and I saw the ice on the deck, and they pointed it out to me: 'Look at that!' they said. 'We have just struck an iceberg.' Then I went down below and woke my two mates up, and then I dressed and walked on the Bridge to await orders from the captain.

After receiving orders to go and prepare boats for launch, William, not knowing his own assigned boat, assisted in loading several boats before sixth officer Jim Moody ordered him to lifeboat 9 to take charge. He got into that boat and assisted women and children aboard. As the boat was lowered, boatswain's mate Albert Haines stepped in and Wynn relinquished charge of the boat to him and manned an oar.

James Witter was on duty in the smoke room at the time of the collision, and at the request of some passengers he went to investigate. Somehow he ended up taking 'Scotland Road', and he encountered a joiner named John Hutchinson, who told him 'The bloody mail room is full'. Then a saloon steward named William Moss told him 'It's really serious, Jim'. He went on deck and helped to load some of the boats. While assisting with lifeboat 11, he stood on the rail trying to help a hysterical woman who was thrashing about, and she lost her footing and fell. Jim grabbed hold of her to stop her fall and they both tumbled into the boat. The officer in command ordered him to remain in the boat, which was in the process of being lowered.

Joe Scarrott worked like mad to get the boats ready for launching:

> The port side boats were got ready first and then the starboard ones. As the work proceeded the passengers were coming on deck with lifebelts on. Then we realised the situation. Every man went to his station. There was no panic, everybody was cool, and when the boats were ready the usual order was given: 'Women and children first.' That order was carried out without any class distinction whatever. In some cases we had to force women into the boat as they would not leave their husbands.
>
> The first boat to leave the ship was full of firemen, but that was because few ladies were willing to go, and it was imperative to fill the boats. The other members of the crew saved were those required to man the boats, and those who saved themselves at the last moment by jumping overboard to chance being able to float until being picked up. Many more could have been saved if the imminence of the danger had been realised at the time of the first alarm.
>
> Why so many ladies hung back at first was because the experience presenting itself was an awesome one, the mere act of getting into the boats being a difficult one, and the long lowering to the water presenting terrifying prospects.

> The men stood back to allow the women to pass, except in one or two cases when men tried to rush, but they were very soon stopped. This occurred at the boat I was in charge of, number 14. About half a dozen foreigners tried to jump in before I had my complement of women and children. They could not understand the orders I gave them, but I drove them back with the boats tiller. One man jumped in twice and I had to throw him out the third time.
>
> Shortly afterwards the fifth officer, Mr Lowe, came and took charge of the boat. I told him what had happened. He drew his revolver and fired two shots between the boat and the ship's side into the water as a warning to any further attempts of that sort. When our boat was lowered we had fifty-four women, four children (one of them a baby in arms), one sailor, two firemen, three stewards, and one officer; total sixty-six souls. There was a man in the boat who we thought was a sailor but he was not. He was a window cleaner (William Harder).

Esther and Eva Hart were put into lifeboat 14, and Esther remembered:

> I know that there was a cry of: 'She's sinking!' I heard hoarse shouts of 'Women and children first,' and then from boat to boat we were hurried, only to be told 'already full'. Four boats we tried, and at the fifth there was room. Eva was thrown in first, and I followed her.
>
> Just then a man who had previously tried to get in, succeeded in doing so, but was ordered out, and the officer fired his revolver into the air to let everyone see it was loaded, and shouted out, 'Stand back, I say, Stand back. The next, man who puts his foot in this boat I will shoot him down like a dog.'

Ben (Mr Hart) – who had been doing what he could to help the women and children, said quietly to the man who had been in charge of the lifeboat, as he gave his coat to Esther to keep her and Eva warm: 'I'm not going in, but for God's sake look after my wife and child.' And little Eva called out to the officer with the revolver: 'Don't shoot my daddy! You shan't shoot my daddy.' Esther continued:

> That was the last I saw of my poor lost dear – no farewell kiss, no fond word – but in a moment, he had gone and we were hanging over the sea, 50 or 60 feet above it, and then there were two or three horrible jerks as the boat was lowered from the davits and we were in the water, so crowded that we could scarcely move. The officer in charge of our boat was standing on that raised part of it right at the end. We were all women and children aboard (at least I thought so then, but we were not, as I will presently tell you), and we were all crying and sobbing; and the officer said, not roughly, but I think with a kindly desire to keep our minds off the terrible time we had gone through: 'Don't cry, please, don't cry. You'll have something else to do than cry; some of you will have to handle the oars. For God's sake, stop crying. If I had not the responsibility of looking after you I would put a bullet through my brain.'

Mary Davison* and her husband, Harry*, were on their way to Cleveland in Ohio, which was fast becoming an important industrial centre, and where Mary had family she hoped to reunite with. She did not agree that there was no sense of urgency among the passengers:

> We had retired when the crash came. Harry threw on some clothing and started on deck to see what was the matter. As we came on the deck we saw man and women fighting about the lifeboats. Some of the boats were lowered and everyone was shouting and pushing about the boat. Harry pulled me into a crowd that was struggling about one of the boats that was being loaded. One of the officers kept crying, 'Women first, get back, women first.' Then someone grabbed me and threw me into the boat (number 16). I was terribly excited and didn't notice how many boats were left, but as we were being lowered I saw other boats pulling off under us and I heard shouts from other boats that seemed a long way out. As we came to the water I heard something whirl over us and strike the water. It was a man. The boat was crowded, there being thirty-five and we couldn't turn around to go back. Some were standing up and as we pushed off the boat listed and took water.

Joseph Hyman also witnessed some of the panic, and he decided to take his chance to get into a lifeboat:

> The forward deck was jammed with people, all of them pushing, and clawing and fighting, and so I walked forward and stepped over the end of the boat that was being got ready and sat down [Collapsible lifeboat C, at about 1:40 am]. Nobody disturbed me, and then a line of men gathered along the side and only opened when a woman or a child came forward. When a man tried to get through he would be pushed back …
>
> There was not much panic before we left, except when the chief officer fired into a belligerent group of third class passengers. A man standing next to him had his chin shot off.
>
> More than one hundred passengers who found seats in lifeboats were drowned when the boats struck the water and capsized. One boat, containing fifty persons, lowered down the side of the great vessel, but before it reached the water the stern tackle caught and the boat struck the water bow first, throwing the shrieking passengers, mostly women, into the water.
>
> Among the third class passengers the confidence in the strength of *Titanic* was so great that even when the officers began to fill the lifeboats there was no panic. The terror did not begin until the lurch of the vessel showed that it was sinking. Then came two explosions, the last of which blew hundreds of persons off into the sea, maiming them and making their fight for life impossible. From the time the lights went out until the vessel plunged head first into the icy sea, there was one prolonged cry as of a single, mighty animal in mortal agony.
>
> When we were nearly to the water we passed a big hole in the side of the boat. This was about three quarters of the way back toward the stern and the pumps were throwing a great stream of water out through it. It threatened to swamp our boat, and we got scared. There were about ten men in the boat and we each took an oar and pushed the boat away from the side of the ship. That's all that saved us.

As the desperate situation began to unfold, the band got together in the first-class lounge and began to play popular ragtime tunes to try to keep the passengers' spirits up as they realised the grave danger they were in. However, when the situation became more serious and the angle of the ship more perilous, they moved out onto the boat deck. As the lifeboats were being loaded and lowered down to the water they changed to playing hymns, and continued to do so with complete disregard for their own safety. It was reported that their last hymn was *Nearer, My God, to Thee*, before they were swamped, and the entire band was swept away by a sudden wave as *Titanic* made its last plunge, and they were all hurled to a pitiless death.

Hilda Slater was on the last lifeboat to pull off:

> Of all the heroes who went to their death when Titanic dived to its ocean grave, none deserved greater credit than the members of the vessel's orchestra. The orchestra played until the last. When the vessel took its final plunge the strains of a lively air, mingled gruesomely with the cries of those who realised that they were face to face with death. From the moment the vessel struck, or as soon as the members of the orchestra could be collected, there was a steady round of lively airs. It did much to keep up the spirits of everyone and probably served as much as the efforts of the officers trying to prevent panic.

Helen Churchill Candee survived the disaster and became a travel writer and explorer. She remembered 'There were no more boats, water was swirling around the upper deck, people were beginning to panic – and the band continued to play.'

Caroline Bonnell stated 'Those that were in the lifeboats who were close to the vessel say that the orchestra played to the very last, and that the men went down into the sea singing *Nearer, My God, to Thee*.'

Kate Gold was in great admiration of the band, 'On deck, the bandsmen were playing ragtime music as the crews were getting out the boats, and it was a noteworthy fact that so interested and engrossed in their duty were these gallant musicians that they would not stop playing to put on life-belts which were brought to them.'

Algernon Barkworth recorded:

> Again, I noticed that the band was playing a waltz tune. Soon afterwards we went to see the boats lowered. The escaping steam making a deafening sound, women and children were put into the boats first. When most of the boats had left the ship, she began to list forward.
>
> Jones and Gee were looking over the side. I learned swimming at Eton and made up my mind if it came to the worst I would try my luck in the water. When the ship gave the first dip we all went aft. Well, I had read somewhere that a ship which is about to sink gives a premonitory dip, and when Titanic did that I simply chucked my despatch case, containing all my money and some papers, into the scuppers, Jones and Gee were standing by, with arms on the rail, looking down. I imagine they were preparing for death.

Harold Bride was still struggling for survival but he too heard the band, although he quoted that they were playing a different tune. 'From aft came the tunes of the band. It was a ragtime tune, I don't know what. Phillips ran aft and that was the last I saw of him alive. The band was still playing. I guess all the band went down. They were heroes. They were still playing *Autumn*.'

Violet Jessop kept her cool:

> I was ordered up on deck. Calmly, passengers strolled about. I stood at the bulkhead with the other stewardesses, watching the women cling to their husbands before being put into the boats with their children. Sometime after, a ship's officer ordered us into the boat (16) first to show some women it was safe. As the boat was being lowered the officer called: 'Here, Miss Jessop, look after this baby.' And a bundle was dropped onto my lap.

Dressed in only her nightgown, Kate Phillips was allocated a place in lifeboat 11, which was the sixth to be lowered. According to a family story, Henry did not want her to go off on her own and tried to cling on to her. However, clutching a brown leather purse with the keys to her trunk, and the precious pendant around her neck, she took her place among other women with their children. Henry was held back, and as he could not swim his prospects of survival were minimal. Although he did not know it, Kate was carrying something of his even more precious than he could have imagined.

One of the sailors noticed her shivering with cold and wrapped his woollen jumper around her to try to keep her warm.

Sarah Stapp was also in lifeboat 11, and she remembered:

> It was a brilliant star-lit night, and Mrs Martin (Kate) was the only woman insufficiently robed. At first she was little inconvenienced, but when the breeze sprang up they had the greatest difficulty in keeping up the circulation in the icy cold.
>
> The crew had the utmost difficulty in trying to persuade the people to get into the boats. It is my own impression that more lives would have been saved if only people could have been persuaded to enter the boats more quickly. I was helped into the last boat but one and had charge of a baby, whose father and mother were lost. There were less than 72 or 77 persons in our boat and I nursed the little mite for several hours. Although the night was starry, it was bitterly cold and everyone was nearly starved.
>
> I think it is most unfair the stories that have been circulated about Mr Ismay. He worked might and main all the time, and I did not think he actually realised the ship was sinking. He helped all he could to get the women into the boats. He implored one group of stewardesses to take their place with the others. The reply was: 'But we are only stewardesses, sir!' When he said: 'You are women. Please get in at once.' And he insisted on their doing so. We saw him later when he was sitting on the gunwale of one of the last boats to leave. He had nothing on but his pyjamas and an overcoat and he was blue with the cold.

Clear and Nellie had been placed into lifeboat 14, which was launched from the aft portside (left rear) of the ship. However, noticing that five lifeboats had left the ship without having an officer in them, Fifth Officer Harold Lowe said to Sixth Officer James Moody 'An officer ought to go in one of these boats,' and asked him who he thought it should be. Officer Moody is said to have told Officer Lowe to get in the boat. Harold Lowe then boarded Lifeboat 14 and assumed command.

Under Harold Lowe's orders, Lifeboat 14 was lowered away from *Titanic* boat deck at around 1.25 am. Fearful of the consequences that might happen if people tried to jump into the lifeboat as it passed the lower decks on its descent to the sea, Harold fired his gun three times alongside the side of the ship to warn people to stay back.

As Lifeboat 14 neared the water a very dangerous situation occurred when, for some reason, the aft end of the lifeboat stopped lowering while the bow continued until it reached the water – causing the stern of the lifeboat to dangle about 5ft in the air. With the stern stuck in the air, the crew aboard the lifeboat were forced to release the ropes attached to the lifeboat to lower it from the ship – causing the lifeboat's stern to come crashing down into the sea. The crash seems to have caused a leak that allowed about 8in of water to fill up the bottom of the lifeboat.

Fred Barrett was among the last of the crew to leave the stricken ship, and he stated:

> When I ran up to the A deck promenade there were only two boats left. I was put in charge of lifeboat 13, which was nearly full when I climbed in, and a few more people got in after me. I heard someone shout from above: 'Let no more in that boat. The falls will break.' The boat was lowered at about twenty minutes to one, and the occupants narrowly avoided a torrent of water from an outfall in the ship's side.

When it had reached the water, Fred had to work quickly to cut the boat free from the falls as it drifted under lifeboat 15, which had begun its descent. There were about seventy souls in the boat, it being so overcrowded that Fred stated that the gunwale was only 6in above the water.

Harold Bride stated:

> I noticed as I came back from one trip that they were putting off women and children in lifeboats. I noticed that the list forward was increasing. Phillips told me that the wireless was growing weaker. The captain came and told us that our engine rooms were taking water and that the dynamos might not last much longer. We sent those facts to the *Carpathia*.
>
> I went on deck and looked around. The water was pretty close up to the boat deck. There was a great scramble aft, and how poor Phillips continued to work through it I don't know. He was a brave man. I learned to love him that night and I suddenly felt a great

> reverence to see him standing there sticking to his work while everybody else was raging about. I will never live to forget the work of Phillips during the last awful fifteen minutes. We picked up the *Olympic* and told her we were sinking by the head.
>
> 'We're about all down.' As Phillips was sending that message I strapped his lifebelt to his back. I had already put on his overcoat, and I wondered if I could get him into his boots. I saw a collapsible boat near the tunnel and went over to it. Twelve men were trying to boost it down to the boat deck. They were having an awful time. It was the last boat left. I looked at it longingly for a few minutes then I gave them a hand. Over she went, and they all started to scramble in. I walked back to Phillips and said: 'The last raft is gone.'

Fred Fleet made his way to the boat deck, where Second Officer Lightoller put him to help Quartermaster Hitchens load and launch lifeboat 6 at 12.55 am, the first boat to be launched from the port side. After loading twenty-eight women and children, the boat was lowered to the water and rowed away from the stricken vessel.

Charles Lightoller ordered a locked-arm circle of crew members around collapsible D so that only women and children could get through, Michel Navratil handed the boys through them, stating to his elder son 'My child, when your mother comes for you, as she surely will, tell her that I loved her dearly, and still do. Tell her I expected her to follow us, so that we might all live happily together in the peace and freedom of the New World.'

Charles remembered:

> Phillips explained when I said that I did not recollect any *Mesaba* report: 'I just put the message under a paper weight at my elbow, just until I squared up what I was doing before sending it to the Bridge.' That delay proved fatal and was the main contributory cause to the loss of that magnificent ship and hundreds of lives. Had I as Officer of the Watch, or the Captain, become aware of the peril lying so close ahead and not instantly slowed down or stopped, we should have been guilty of culpable and criminal negligence.

Harold Bride continued:

> Then came the captain's voice: 'Men, you have done your full duty. You can do no more. Abandon your cabin now. It's every man for himself. You look out for yourselves. I release you.' That's the way of it at this kind of time, every man for himself. I looked out. The boat deck was awash. Phillips clung on, sending – sending. The water was then coming into our cabin while he worked. I looked out. The boat deck was awash. Phillips clung on sending and sending. He clung on for about ten minutes, or maybe fifteen minutes after the captain had released him.

Jack Phillips's last message was picked up by the *Virginian* of the Allen Line at 2.17 am, and *Titanic* foundered at 2.20 am.

6. For Those in Peril

Swept from peace and comfort to an unexpected doom, there must have been many a handshake and many a sobbed farewell, and it is hard to imagine what it must have been like to witness the screams of heartbroken wives as they were taken from the arms of their husbands, and the piteous cries of children who were forced into the boats ready to be rowed away, leaving to a sure and awful death to those who were sacrificed that they might live.

As many people in the lifeboats watched with dread, the listing of the ship became severe, and then it began to lurch forward now and again as the front sank deeper and deeper into the icy water, causing people still on board to cry out with terror. There were several loud explosions, which blew many people overboard and into a watery grave. Finally, the ship plunged downwards and the final cries of the doomed passengers rang out as it simply disappeared beneath the surface.

Esther Hart witnessed the ship go down:

> So we got away from the ship for a safe distance, for there was no doubt now about her sinking. The front portion of her was pointing down wards, and she appeared to be breaking in halves. Then, with a mighty and tearing sob, as of some gigantic thing instinct with life, the front portion of her dived.

Eva Hart added:

> I saw that ship sink. I never closed my eyes. I didn't sleep at all. I saw it, I heard it, and nobody could possibly forget it. I can remember the colours, the sounds, everything. The worst thing I can remember are the screams. It seemed as if once everybody had gone, drowned, finished, the whole world was standing still. There was nothing, just this deathly, terrible silence in the dark night with the stars overhead. The band played one version of *Nearer, My God, To Thee* of which there are three and the one they played

> was the one that was played in church. I never closed my eyes at all – I saw that ship sink. And I saw that ship break in half.

Clear Cameron '... saw the ship split in two and heard two more explosions from beneath the water as she went down. For a few moments it was silent. Then terrible crying arose from the people left behind. This seemed to last for hours.'

Adolphe Saalfeld remembered:

> As we drifted away we gradually saw Titanic sink lower and lower and finally her lights went out, and others in my boat said they saw her disappear. Our boat was nearly two miles away but pitiful cries could be plainly heard. No one in our boat knew how many lifeboats were on Titanic but ... there was ample time for saving every soul on board had there been sufficient boats.

Sarah Stap recalled:

> We could hear the music of the band all the time. They were heroes if you like. I must say that everything that has been said about them is perfectly true. They were not asked to play, but did it absolutely on their own initiative. In fact, from the highest to the lowest member of the crew, every one of them deserves the highest praise.
>
> I would also like to praise the lifebelts. Many people were saved by these. They were not the old-fashioned ones that fastened on the shoulder, but ones to be slipped over the head and tied round the waist.

Joe Scarrott recorded:

> The aft fall got twisted and we dropped the boat by releasing gear and got clear of the ship. When the boat was in the water we rowed clear of the ship. There were four men rowing. We then saw four other boats well clear and fairly well-filled with women and children. We went to them and found none of them had an officer in charge. So the fifth officer took charge of the lot, ordering them to

keep with him. Titanic was then about fifty yards off, and we lay there with the boats. Mr Lowe was at the helm.

The ship sank shortly afterwards, I should say about 2:20am on the 15th, which would be about two hours and forty minutes after she struck. The sight of that grand ship going down will never be forgotten. She slowly went down bow first with a slight list to starboard until the water reached the bridge then she went quicker. When the third funnel had nearly disappeared I heard four explosions, which I took to be the bursting of the boilers. The ship was right up on end then. Suddenly she broke in two between the third and fourth funnel. The after part of the ship came down on the water in its normal position and seemed as if it was going to remain afloat, but it only remained a minute or two and then sank. The lights were burning right up until she broke in two. The cries from the poor souls struggling in the water seemed terrible in the stillness of the night. It seemed to go through you like a knife.

Our officer (Lowe) then ordered all the boats under his charge to row towards where the ship went down to see if we could pick up anybody. Some of our boats picked up a few. I cannot say how many. After that we tied all our boats together so as to form a large object on the water which would be seen quicker than a single boat by a passing vessel. We divided the passengers of our boat amongst the other four, and then taking one man from each boat so as to make a crew we rode away amongst the wreckage as we heard cries for help coming from that direction.

When we got to it the sight we saw was awful. We were amongst hundreds of dead bodies floating in lifebelts. We could only see four alive. The first one we picked up was a male passenger. He died shortly after we got him in the boat. After a hard struggle we managed to get the other three. One of these we saw kneeling as if in prayer upon what appeared to be a part of a staircase. He was only about twenty yards away from us but it took us half-an-hour to push our boat through the wreckage and bodies to get to him; even then we could not get very close, so we put out an oar for him to get hold of and so pulled him to the boat. All the bodies we saw seemed as if they had perished with the cold as their limbs were all cramped up. As we left that awful scene we gave way to tears. It was enough to break the stoutest heart.

Evelyn Marsden* had learned to row on the Murray River in Australia and she was able to put her skills to good use as she helped to get lifeboat 16 away from the stricken ship.

Algernon Barkworth put his swimming skills to good use:

> I had on a fur coat with the lifebelt strapped to the outside … [stating later that it made him look like 'some waterlogged sheepdog']. When I came up, I swam for all I was worth to get away from the sinking ship.
>
> Coming across a floating plank, I rested upon it. Looking over my should I saw Titanic disappear with a volley of loud reports, so I swam slowly around and came luckily upon an overturned lifeboat (collapsible B). I climbed upon this at this time. The screams of the drowning was most terrible. Several more people climbed up the stern of the boat, which was now full. We competed to keep everyone else from gathering upon.

Harold Bride had to do some quick thinking:

> I went to the place I had seen the collapsible boat on the boat deck, and to my surprise I saw the boat and the men still trying to push it off. I guess there wasn't a sailor in the crowd. They couldn't do it. I went up to them and was just lending a hand when a large wave came awash of the deck. The big wave carried the boat off. I had hold of an oar-lock and I went off with it. The next I knew I was in the boat.
>
> But that was not all. I was in the boat and the boat was upside down and I was under it. I remember I realised I was wet through, and whatever happened I must not breathe, for I was under water.
>
> I knew I had to fight for it and I did. How I got out from under the boat I do not know, but I felt a breath of air at last.
>
> There were men all around me – hundreds of them. The sea was dotted with them, all depending on their lifebelts.

> I felt I simply had to get away from the ship. She was a beautiful sight then. Smoke and sparks were rushing out of her funnel. There must have been an explosion, but we heard none. We only saw the big stream of sparks. The ship was gradually turning on her nose, just like a duck does that goes down for a dive. I had only one thing on my mind – to get away from the suction.
>
> Then I swam with all my might. I suppose I was 150 feet [in another statement he said 60 yards] away when Titanic, on her nose, with her after-quarter sticking straight up into the air, began to settle slowly. When at last the waves washed over her rudder there wasn't the least bit of suction I could feel. She must have kept going down just as flowing as she had been. That was her end.
>
> I felt after a little while like sinking. I was very cold. I saw a boat of some kind near me, and put all my strength into an effort to swim to it. It was hard work, and I was all alone when a hand reached out from the boat and pulled me aboard. It was our same collapsible boat and the same crowd was on it.
>
> There was just room for me to roll on the edge. I lay there not caring what happened. Somebody sat on my legs. They were wedged in between slats and were being wrenched. I had not the heart to ask the man to move. It was a terrible sight all round – men swimming and sinking. I lay where I was, letting the man wrench my feet out of shape. Others came near. Nobody gave them a hand. The bottom-up boat already had more men than it would hold and it was sinking.

Fred Barrett took the tiller and steered it away from the stricken ship. He was only wearing light clothing designed to work in the hot boiler rooms and he became too cold to continue the task. A woman put a shawl around his shoulders and he fell asleep until the lifeboat was brought safely to the side of *Carpathia* at a quarter to five in the morning.

Sarah Stap was haunted by what she witnessed and heard:

> I shall never forget it until my dying day. There we were all huddled up together. It was awful, we could see the lights of the ship slowly disappearing beneath the waves, one by one, until there alone remained the mast light. Then suddenly the great ship gave a lurch

> and disappeared gracefully out of sight. All this time the people on board were shrieking in their death agonies, and the passengers were under the impression that it was the other people in the boats cheering. Only the members of the crew knew what it was and we dared not say. After the ship had gone an explosion rent the air. The shrieks of the dying were positively awful. During the time we were in the lifeboat we passed about six or seven icebergs.

Joseph Hyman knew it was essential that they got away from the sinking ship as soon as possible:

> When we settled into the water we pulled away like mad, because we didn't know whether *Titanic* would sink or not and were afraid of the suction. When we were about fifty yards away I noticed that the portholes forward were lower than those aft, and then got my first impression that the ship was sinking. When we had pulled further away I saw the iceberg. It was black and was about fifty yards astern.
>
> We pulled away about half a mile and then rested and watched. One by one I saw the forward portholes go out, just like someone was walking back through the ship and turning out the electric lights. Then we heard a small explosion and a terrible cry. The cry was blood curdling and never stopped until Titanic went down, when it seemed to be sort of choked off. The cry is ringing in my ears now and always will. We sat there silent, we were terror stricken.
>
> In less than ten minutes there came an explosion, and I could see men, women and pieces of the ship blown into the air from the after deck. I saw bodies partly blown to pieces floating around, and I am sure more than a hundred persons were blown off into the sea by that explosion. I met one man on the Carpathia who was blown off, but caught a piece of a table and floated.
>
> At the second explosion the lights went out. Even the lights on the masthead went out. And everything was dark for a few moments. A terrible hissing of steam began and the awful cry went on. I tried to close my ears, but there was some mysterious attraction and I had to hear that cry.

When my eyes got used to the dark I could make out Titanic, still with the front part down in the water. That was about half-past one, I guess. The hissing and screaming kept up, and finally the ship seemed to right itself, then suddenly the front end plunged down and she sank like a stone. The cry was choked off, and the hissing of steam stopped, but the sudden silence was almost more terrifying than the screams. We didn't feel the suction, except for a big wave that rocked our boat about two minutes after.

After the lifeboat in which we left *Titanic* put out some distance, shrill cries and screams could be heard distinctly.

Alice Phillips was alarmed to see the boat sinking, and to know that her father was still on board was too terrible to think of … 'I cannot forget the awful cries of those poor people who perished. It was simply awful!'

Tom Whiteley got away from the stricken vessel and watched her go down:

In some way I got overboard myself and found something to hold on to – an oak dresser about the size of this hospital bed. I wasn't more than sixty feet from Titanic when she went down. I was aft and could see her big stern rise up in the air as she went down bow first. I saw the machinery drop out of her. I was in the water about half an hour and could hear the cries of thousands of people, it seemed. Then I drifted near a boat wrong side up. About thirty men were clinging to it. They refused to let me get on. Someone tried to hit me with an oar, but I scrambled on to her.

Phillips, the first Marconi operator, stuck to his post till the last. He was on the overturned lifeboat with me and was dead when they took him aboard the Carpathia. They tried to revive him with brandy and all that, but it was too late. There were four burials at sea on the *Carpathia* – one sailor, two firemen and Phillips. When I last saw the captain he was in the water trying to place a baby in one of the lifeboats crowded with people. Some women tried to drag him on the boat, but he pulled away from them and said: 'Save yourselves.' I saw him go under, and he never came up.

The Bonnell ladies were placed in lifeboat 8, which was one of the first to leave the ship, and Caroline continued:

In the lifeboats it was terrible. Some of the women had scarcely any clothes on at all, and they suffered greatly with the cold. One woman had light satin slippers and an evening dress on. I don't know whether she had that attire on when we struck, or whether, in her excitement, she put it on by mistake.

We were provided with the most miserable little oil lamps I have ever seen. I guess it didn't have any kerosene in it, for it kept going out as fast as we could light it with the matches which the steward happened to bring along. We couldn't have seen at all nor signalled had it not been for the fact that one woman had a cane that had a little electric light in the end of it. As far as I know there was no food or water in the craft, but I will not complain of that for we were the luckiest, I guess, of all the survivors. The other boats all leaked, and the women told us afterwards that the water was up to their knees. And that water was below freezing point, 31 degrees to be even.

Lifeboat 14 had met up with Lifeboats 4, 10, 12 and Collapsible D. Officer Lowe decided that his boat should return to the site of the wreck to try to rescue survivors. He began to transfer all the passengers out of Lifeboat 14 into the other lifeboats in the group. As the woman and children were being transferred, Harold was unimpressed to find that there was a man in the boat disguised as a woman, so he 'pitched' him into the other lifeboat. Two crewmen were transferred from Lifeboat 10 into Lifeboat 14.

Tom Threlfall was in lifeboat 14, and recalled:

Then he (Officer Lowe) called to several other boats close by, 'Throw out your painters,' and we linked them all up. Mr Lowe passed about fifty women and children from his boat, and said, 'We will go for the wreckage', to which other people were clinging. From the wreckage we picked up four men. Then Mr. Lowe called out, 'There's a boat over there and she's sinking.' Although we were then towing a collapsible boat with about eighty people in her we reached the sinking boat just as the water was up to her gunwale and took twenty-six men and one woman, a Mrs Abbott, off her. I held the woman in my arms till we reached *Carpathia*.

Clear Cameron noted:

> Officer Lowe decided to go back to search for survivors, and transferred all the passengers from lifeboat 14 into lifeboat 10. According to Nellie a 'madman' kept shaking the boat and they feared it would capsize, so he was pushed overboard. Lifeboat 14 was reportedly the only one which went back to look for survivors and six victims were pulled from the water, but two of them died.

After Harold had allowed a first-class passenger named Charles Williams into the boat to help to row, some people expressed a fear that they might be swamped by desperate people if they returned, so Harold reluctantly agreed to wait until the screams from those in peril had died down a bit before he went back to help the drowning passengers. Lifeboat 14 made the journey of approximately 150 yards back to the wreck site, and when they arrived at the wreckage they were confronted with the dreadful sight of countless dead bodies floating in the icy water.

The first man they rescued was a first-class passenger named William Hoyt. The crew grappled him aboard, and they did their best to help him but he was too far gone and he soon died. His body was taken to *Carpathia*, from where he was buried at sea. Two further passengers rescued included a man who seems to have been an Oriental third-class passenger named Fang Lang.

The final person to be rescued was a steward named Harold Phillimore, who was clinging to the top of some wreckage that looked like a piece of staircase. They had to push their way through many dead bodies to get to him. On holding out an oar for him to grab, they saw that he was too frozen to grasp it and had to go closer to him so they could haul him into the boat.

After rescuing all the survivors they could find in the water, Harold constructed a makeshift sail that allowed them to make more progress. As they did so, they saw Collapsible D and sailed towards it. A rope was thrown to the vessel and it was taken in tow.

On the way to *Carpathia*, Collapsible A was noticed in the distance, stranded and appearing to be sinking. Clinging to life on board were around thirteen survivors.

Harold Lowe was instrumental in saving the lives of at least fifty-seven people: forty on his lifeboat, four from the wreckage, and thirteen from Collapsible A.

Mary Davison in lifeboat 16 noted:

> It was frightfully cold and all the women in the boat were scantily clothed. Nearly all were women and there were only three sailors. Some of the women tried to help the sailors to row, but we didn't make much headway. It seemed hours before Titanic sank, but we had not gone far away. Its stern came up ... then there was an explosion. The cold was intense. We were afraid to move for fear of sinking the boat. Water kept coming into it until there were several inches on the bottom. Ice bumped against us at times. It seemed dawn would never come. The sailors kept rowing all night. The strain was terrible. A woman fainted and a man began to laugh and sob toward morning.

Esther Hart continued her story:

> An inky blackness now settled over us, and not a soul in our boat had a match; but the officer found in his pockets an electric torch, which he kept flashing, shouting out all the time, 'Keep together – it's our only chance'.
>
> The duty that the officer allotted to me was to bale the water out of the boat. While sitting there I had the impression that there was somebody near me who ought not to be there. So, when I could get my elbows free I put my hand down under the seat and touched a human form.
>
> It was a poor wretch of a man who had smuggled himself into the boat and had sat there all that time under the seat in about six inches of water. When we got him out he was so stiff he could scarcely move.
>
> It had got a little lighter now and our officer had collected nearly all the boats together, and he called from one to the other: 'How many in yours? How many in yours?' and then he discovered that, there was room in the other boats to put the whole of our 55 in, so we were transferred to them, and the officer now collected a few seamen in his now empty boat and hewed away to see what he could find. So, with proper management, another 55 people could have been saved.

Joseph Hyman was in collapsible C, and remembered:

> The women were crying, but the men in our boat were still. We rowed about for a while to try and find the other boats and finally came upon four more. We also found a lot of men floating around on tables and chairs but had no room to pick up any of them. One man had tied three deck chairs together and was floating all night.
>
> Some of the men in our boat took off their coats and threw them around the women, who were almost frozen. The wind began to blow sharply, and the boat started rocking a little, but the sea was never dangerous.
>
> In about two hours we saw a glint of light off to the west. We watched it for an hour, and then we could see that there were two lights and it must be a ship, so we rowed toward it. The exercise kept us men warm, but the women, most of them first cabin passengers, were nearly frozen to death.
>
> I don't recall being afraid, I remember the pleasure, really, of going plop! into the lifeboat. We ended up next to the daughter of an American banker who managed to save her dog – no one objected. There were vast differences of people's wealth on the ship, and I realised later that if we hadn't been in second-class, we'd have died. The people who came out alive often cheated and were aggressive. The honest didn't stand a chance.

Harry Eches in lifeboat 5 remembered how he rowed as hard as he could to get away from the dangerous suction of the sinking vessel. He stated later:

> We laid off about 100 yards from the ship and waited. She seemed to be going down at the head and we pulled away about a quarter of a mile and laid on out oars until *Titanic* sank. She seemed to rise once as though she was going to take a final dive, but sort of checked as though she had scooped the water up and had levelled herself. She then seemed to settle very, very quietly, until the last, when she rose and seemed to stand twenty seconds, stern in that position (here he indicated with his arm) and then she went down with an awful grating, like a small boat running off a shingly beach. There was no inrush of water, or anything.

Mr Pitman then said to pull back to the scene of the wreck. The ladies started calling out. Two ladies sitting in front where I was pulling said: 'Appeal to the officer not to go back. Why should we lose all our lives in a useless attempt to save others from the ship?

We did not go back. When we left ship number 5 had forty-two, including the children, six crew, and the officer. Two were transferred with a lady and a child into boat number 7.

Charles Andrews remembered:

> Besides these six men, I should think there were about fifty passengers. There was no effort on the part of the steerage men to get into our boat. I was told by the officer to allow none in it. When the officer started to fill the boat with passengers, and the men to man it, there were no individuals who tried to get in, or that he permitted to get in. There was no confusion whatever. After they were all in the boat the officer looked around at me and asked me if I could take an oar, and I said I could, sir. At that he told me to get into the boat. After I got in the boat I assisted by putting the rowlocks in. We lowered the boat to the water and rowed away from the ship. On our way out we ... had to rest because we came across another boat, sir, filled up with ladies. The remark was passed by someone in the boat to go back, but as the two boats were full we stood at a distance away.

While manning the tiller of lifeboat 6, Quartermaster Hitchens, who, even in their perilous situation was overly pessimistic, constantly beat back attempts by those on the boat to return to pick up survivors, saying they would only find 'stiffs'. He also yelled at the rowers, saying they would be drifting for days, and that any rescue ship was only coming to pick up bodies. 'The Unsinkable' Molly Brown threatened to toss him overboard after this argument, as a result of which the women rowed around looking for survivors, but found none.

In number 11 boat there were seventy-five people, sixty-two being women. After pulling away from the side of Titanic it was found two German males had concealed themselves in the boat before it was lowered. They were found under the seats, and one of them refused to come out, wrapping Mrs Gold's skirts around him to keep warm. One of the crew prodded him several times with an oar yet failed to induce him to budge an inch. His compatriot did take his share of work at the oar, but the skulking fellow was permanently idle, except when he was once heard counting out his money.

Kate Gold recalled:

> One of the sailors caused the only laugh that was heard in the boat when, as a bird rose from the water, he facetiously said: 'I like a bird that sings in the morning!'
>
> We did not talk very much, and almost the only sounds we had to attract our attention were the cries of the babies in the boat. This was, of course, after we had heard the last of the despairing shrieks of those who went down in the liner and those who were left swimming in the water when she disappeared.
>
> The behaviour of the older children in the lifeboat was splendid, and they were a great consolation to the women.

7. 'Save Our Souls!'

It is hard to imagine how the survivors must have felt. Many of them harboured helpless guilt at having left their loved ones behind. The sea was calm, but it was dark, and they had no way of knowing if rescue ships had been made aware of the disaster. Even if they had, would they be found before they froze or died of thirst and hunger?

While he was manning his lifeboat, William Wynn reported seeing 'red and white lights off into the distance, and soon the red light disappeared'.

He took the lights to be the port lights of a steamer about seven or eight miles away. In the boat they had no lamp to see and no compass to guide them, and no oil.

Eva Hart believed that she had seen a ship in close proximity to the sinking, and believed that it was SS *Californian*. She stated in later life:

> I saw that ship. It was terribly close. I didn't see a ship nineteen miles away, I saw a ship that was so close; and they said at the time it was less than nine miles away; now they're trying to say it was nineteen. I saw it you know, and it wasn't just lights on the horizon – you could see it was a ship. And I saw our rockets being fired, which that ship must have seen. Well, this inquiry says that they did see it but they didn't think it was a portent of danger. I would have thought in the middle of the Atlantic in the middle of the night that rockets must mean trouble.

Esther Hart remembered:

> So there we sat the weary night through, until at eight in the morning the *Carpathia* came on the scene. I always thought that these ship boats had to be provisioned beforehand, in view of possible accidents, but there was no water nor were there biscuits, in the boat. An oversight, I suppose; but one fraught with terrible consequences had not the *Carpathia* arrived in good time.

Unfortunately, three men on lifeboat 14 died during the night. When *Carpathia* arrived, the Collapsible B was slowly sinking, and as *Carpathia* was picking up other survivors the men on the capsized boat transferred to lifeboat 12, which was the last boat to be rescued.

Joe Scarrott expressed his relief when he realised that they were going to be rescued:

> Just then we sighted the lights of a steamer, which proved to be the steamship *Carpathia* of the Cunard Line. What a relief that was. We then made sail and went back to our other boats. By this time day was just beginning to dawn. We then saw we were surrounded by icebergs and field ice. Some of the fields of ice were from sixteen to twenty miles long. On our way back we saw one of our collapsible boats waterlogged; there were about eighteen persons on it, so we went and took them off. We left two dead bodies on it, and were told two others had died and had fallen off.

A *Carpathia* spokesman reported the scene as they arrived at the area where Titanic went down:

> The Sea was dotted with bodies as far as one could see, and the decks were covered with them. Everybody had on a lifebelt and bodies floated very high in the water in spite of the sodden clothes and things in pockets. Apparently the people who had? lots of time and discipline must have been splendid, for some had on their pyjamas, two and three shirts, two pairs of pants, two vests, two jackets and an overcoat. In some pockets a quantity of meat and biscuits were found, while in the pockets of most of the crew quite a lot of tobacco and matches besides keys to the various lockers and stateroom doors were found. On this day we buried fifteen bodies some of them very badly smashed and bruised.

Joe Scarrott continued:

> All our boats proceeded towards *Carpathia*. She had stopped right over where our ship had gone down. She had got our wireless message for assistance. When we got alongside we were got aboard as

soon as possible. We found some survivors had already been picked up. Everything was in readiness for us – dry clothes, blankets, beds, hot coffee, spirits, etc, everything to comfort us.

I must say that the passengers when they were in the boats, especially the women, were brave and assisted the handling of the boats a great deal. Thank God the weather was fine or I do not think there would have been one soul left to tell the tale.

The last of the survivors were got aboard about 8:30am. The dead bodies that were in some of the boats were taken aboard and after identification were given a proper burial. There were two male passengers, one fireman and one able seaman.

We steamed about in the vicinity for a few hours in the hope of finding some more survivors, but we did not find any. During that time wives were enquiring for husbands, sisters for brothers, and children for their parents, but many a sad face told the result.

The *Carpathia* was bound from New York to Gibraltar, but the captain decided to return to New York with us. We arrived there about nine pm on Thursday the 18th. We had good weather during the trip, but it was a sad journey. A list of the survivors was taken as soon as we had left the scene of the disaster.

On arrival at New York everything possible was ready for our immediate assistance – clothing, money, medical aid and good accommodation. In fact, I think it would have been impossible for the people of America to have treated us better.

Algernon Barkworth in Collapsible B was still worried about the precarious situation as his vessel was taking on water:

We drifted until daybreak when we sighted the *Carpathia* about five miles off. Shortly after that we got near to *Titanic* lifeboat, which rescued us from our perilous position. With daylight, a strong breeze arose which threatened to submerge us. When we were rescued the water was up to our knees. We had two dead men on our stern, one of which fell off. The other one was taken aboard Carpathia and was afterwards buried (at sea). When taken aboard we were treated most kindly.

Harold Bride was close to giving up all hope of rescue:

> I saw some lights off in the distance and knew a steam ship was coming to our aid. I didn't care what happened. I just lay and gasped when I could, and felt the pain in my feet. I feel it still.
>
> At last the *Carpathia* was alongside, and the people were being taken up by a rope ladder. Our boat drew near, and one by one the men were taken off.
>
> One man was dead. I passed him and went up the ladder, although my feet pained terribly. The dead man was Phillips. He had died on the raft from exposure and cold. I guess he had been all in from work before the wreck came. He stood his ground until the crisis had passed, and then he collapsed, I guess. But I hardly thought that then. I didn't think much of anything. I tried the rope ladder. My feet pained terribly, but I got to the top and felt hands reaching out for me.
>
> The next I knew a woman was leaning over me in a cabin and I felt her hand waving back my hair and rubbing my face. I felt somebody at my feet, and felt the warmth of liquor. Somebody got me under the arms, and then I was carried down below to the hospital.
>
> That was early in the day. I guess I lay in the hospital until near night, when they told me the *Carpathia* wireless man was acting 'queer' and would I help?
>
> After that I never was out of the wireless room, so I don't know what happened to the passengers.

Harold discovered that the wireless man was his old friend Harold Cottam, whose endeavours to send countless personal messages from the survivors to their loved ones had exhausted him, so they worked together in the task.

Arthur Rostron, the captain of *Carpathia,* stated:

> Our passengers saw the survivors required dry and warm clothing, so off they took them to their own cabins to fit them out with everything they could. All our men passengers gave up their cabins, and many of the women doubled up with others so as to leave their own quarters free for the distressed. Every officer, of course, yielded his accommodation.

Caroline Bonnell described how she was taken on board the rescue ship:

> It wasn't long before they let down a little wooden seat [from the *Carpathia*] about two feet long and a foot wide. Men on the deck held the ends of the cables to which this seat was attached. The lifeboat was bobbing up and down on the waves and it was pretty hard to stand up in it long enough to climb out to the seat, but you can wager we all did it.
>
> After we picked up all the lifeboats we steamed again about the scene of the disaster. In among the glassy, towering peaks of ice we threaded our way, seeing a bit of wreckage here and a baby's bonnet or a man's glove there, but no boats, and at noon we turned toward Ambrose lightship and home.
>
> The distress of Titanic survivors secured for them every concession from the passengers of the Carpathia. Women and men alike gave up their staterooms to us and slept on the floors of the library and smoking room. Mrs John Jacob Astor was given one of the best rooms in the cabin and she never emerged from it during the trip. Everyone on the *Carpathia* was kindness itself. Captain Rostron, the surgeon, the stewards, everyone could not do enough for us; and to think that Nathalie and I wished to see the iceberg all the way over.

When daylight came Clear Cameron saw six large icebergs, and they were picked up by the *Carpathia* at a quarter-to-seven, and found they had to sleep on the tables of the dining saloon; but at least they were alive.

Joseph Hyman stated:

> We did not see the *Carpathia* until just before the sun was rising. With regard to the treatment of survivors on the *Carpathia*, it was mentioned that the stewardesses had to sleep on deck as there was no other accommodation for them, but some of the passengers of the *Carpathia* came out of their own rooms to enable Titanic passengers to have use of their rooms.
>
> As soon as it got light we could see that the ship was the Carpathia, and we reached it in another hour. We had to be lifted aboard, as some of the women were unconscious. They gave us coffee and brandy and we felt better.

After I was taken aboard the Carpathia, one capsized boat, with a steward riding astride the keel, was picked up, and the steward confirmed what I had seen. Three empty boats were picked up, riding right side up, but empty.

There were boats coming towards the Carpathia from all sides; in some were men and women badly mangled. They had to be lifted aboard on stretchers, and if it hadn't been so calm they could never have gotten aboard at all.

Carpathia stood by for four hours, then another ship came up. I don't know the name of it. They signalled to each other, and then began to take a big circle, one on each side. The circle was about twenty miles across and in the middle was a big ice floe, fully ten miles wide, but I don't think it was the one Titanic struck. We picked up altogether sixteen boats; besides those we found three empty ones, and one had been capsized, with a man floating on top.

Carpathia then came back to where Titanic sank. You could tell the place by the corks, boxes, bottles, chairs and things floating around on the water, and now and then a big cloud of bubbles would come up. Then we turned and made for New York.

Alice Phillips expressed her relief:

After drifting around for nine hours, almost frozen with the intense cold, we were rescued by the *Carpathia*. I cannot tell you the joy we felt when we were safely on the boat. We had hot coffee and brandy, which warmed us. We were sleeping in the smoke-room on the floor or anywhere, and were only too thankful to do so! … One of the stewards on the *Carpathia* gave me a dollar to spend. It was very good of him.

Sarah Stap was also thankful to be saved:

We were at length picked up by the *Carpathia* and taken to New York. The people on board were ever so kind to us. When we reached New York we were given clothes and every attention, and were then transferred to the Lapland and arrived at Plymouth last

> Sunday morning. All the officers and officials of the White Star Company were extremely kind to us all the time. I had no time to gather up my belongings and so lost everything. But what I valued most was the loss of dear kind friends who went down with the ship. I shall never forget the experience, never!

Violet Jessop stated:

> I was still clutching the baby against my hard cork lifebelt I was wearing when a woman leaped at me and grabbed the baby and rushed off with it. It appeared that she put it down on the deck of Titanic while she went off to fetch something, and when she came back the baby had gone. I was too frozen and numb to think it strange that this woman had not stopped to say 'Thank You.'

Adolph Saalfeld:

> The Captain and officers of the *Carpathia* did all that was possible to make us comfortable and to those that were sick or injured, they gave their tenderest care. The icebergs were huge and the weather extremely rough on the voyage to New York.

Tom Whiteley noted the time he was rescued: 'At 8:40 o'clock in the morning we were taken aboard the *Carpathia*.'

8. Aftermath

Families and friends of the victims read conflicting reports concerning the sinking of *Titanic* on the day after the disaster, which could only have added to their confusion and stress:

> MAMMOTH OCEAN LINER IN DISTRESS
> The Titanic Sinking
> Three Thousand People on Board
> Monday, 15 April
>
> The White Star liner, *Titanic*, the largest vessel in the world, struck an iceberg off Newfoundland, and is in a sinking condition.
>
> A wireless message states that assistance is needed. A vessel has gone to her aid.
>
> A later message states that the women and children are being taken off first.
>
> There are three thousand people on board.
>
> It is reported that the crippled steamer *Titanic* is steaming slowly in the direction of Halifax.
>
> Various liners have recently encountered an ice-field a hundred miles long and twenty-five miles broad off the coast of Newfoundland, which has made the voyages perilous.
>
> Later Particulars
> *Titanic* Reported to have Sunk
> Terrible Loss of Life Feared
>
> News has reached London that *Titanic* has sunk, and that 679 lives have been saved. It is feared that many passengers perished.
>
> OCEAN DISASTER
> TITANIC SINKING

OVER 600 PERSONS SAVED
New York, April 15

The White Star Atlantic liner *Titanic*, inward bound, has sent out wireless messages intimating that she has collided with an iceberg, and is in need of assistance.
The Allan liner *Virginian* is hastening to her aid.
April 15, 10 a.m.

The Titanic is off Cape Race, the south-east point of Newfoundland. She is sinking by the head. The women are being taken off. There are nearly 3000 souls on board.

This is the maiden voyage of the *Titanic*, which left Southampton on Wednesday.

The *Titanic* struck the iceberg on Sunday evening.

She has 1380 passengers on board, including 300 in the first-class, and her crew totals 650.

The *Virginian* received the *Titanic*'s appeals for assistance when 170 miles off.

The White Star liners *Olympic* and *Baltic* have gone to the rescue.

It is doubtful, however, whether the vessels will arrive in time, as the last wireless signals from the *Titanic* were blurred and ended abruptly.

It was learned from the messages that were received that the women and children had left the ship in the life boats.

The weather at the time of the disaster was calm.

The passengers include Mr W T Stead, the well-known journalist; Mr James Ismay, of Ismay, Imrie, and Co, owners of the While Star Line; Colonel J Astor, and several New York bankers.

The largest contingent of victims came from Southampton. It was the hometown of most of the crew, and as many as 500 households in the town lost at least one family member or lodger. Liverpool was also badly affected by the enormous loss of life of people from that city, and the disaster cast a shadow over most areas of Britain in some way or another.

The young boxers Dai Bowen and Leslie Williams were lost in the sinking, and Charles Barnett reported:

Fred Dyer has felt this most deeply, and tells us that he had a weird telepathic (he supposes) experience of the disaster. He woke on the fatal Monday morning with a feeling of suffocation and all the sensations of drowning. He knew that he was wide awake, but could not stir for nearly 30 minutes. He assures us that his nerves are still suffering from the shock of that awful experience, although it was not until he learnt the full details of the tragedy that he associated the events in his mind.

On the very day the news of the disaster came through I received a letter from Mr Frank Torreyson, who held the [boxers'] contract, saying that he was hurrying from Braddock to New York to meet the lads. 'I will keep them in New York for a couple of days,' he said, 'so that they shall enjoy the sights. The season here is drawing to a close, but even if they fail to get a match I will look after them.

That brief epistle will give you some idea of the sport Mr Torreyson is, and I can assure you that I am deeply pained by the tragic occurrence. I treat it as a personal blow, for I had hoped for great things being accomplished by these poor fellows, and the relatives and friends of the pair were equally confident.

The *Southport Guardian* noted:

When the terrible news of the fatal accident to the great sea giant who started so happily on her maiden voyage so lately, our prayers and thoughts were especially with one of the passengers, Miss Lily Bonnell, of Welbeck Road, Birkdale, and our sympathies went out to her two sisters in their awful anxiety and grief ... Hundreds of anxious hearts are praying to God for the news of her safety.

We little thought that within a few hours' time she would be tossing about in a lifeboat at the mercy of wind and wave, and we trust that they will soon hear of her safety.

Ben and Ellen Howard's daughter waited anxiously for news of their fate:

This news, coming so suddenly and unexpectedly, has been a terrible shock; but we hope for the best. But it is terribly? hard having to wait in uncertainty – with this awful suspense. We were more hopeful last night when we heard all the passengers were saved, but now 800 out of 2000 are not many.

Alice Phillips told of the disaster and warned her family about future travel:

I expect you have read of the awful wreck of *Titanic*, and have seen my name on the list of survivors? I expect you have. Oh, I cannot tell you how dreadful it was. My darling father has perished in the wreck, and I feel almost out of my mind with grief. You know how good he was to me, so you can imagine just what I feel like. It seems almost too hard to bear, dear.

I cannot give you a full account of everything that happened. It would take too long to tell, but I will try to describe something of it.

We reached New York on Thursday evening, and my uncle was there to meet me. I cannot tell you how pleased I was to see him. We stayed at the *Strand Hotel* for the night, and the next day a lady, who is named Mrs Longstaffe, came and enquired for me, and took us to her home for the day, and provided me with some clothes. I lost everything I possessed, and I had not a penny to call my own.

If you ever come to America, dear, don't come in a big boat, as I don't think they are as safe as the small ones … I am here with my aunt and uncle now, and I think, when I have got over the grief, I shall be quite happy with them.'

Titanic disaster meant that other events of the day were pushed to the back pages of all the newspapers. Harriet Quimby was the first woman to gain a pilots' licence in the United States, and on 16 April 1912 she became the first woman to pilot an aircraft across the English Channel. However, her pioneering feat received little media attention. A few weeks later she plunged 1000 feet from a plane to her death.

Another event that happened on that date was a report from official sources that Pope Pius X had died suddenly. Newspapers had published long obituary notices and bells of Catholic churches tolled. This news also went virtually unnoticed, which in this case was fortunate as the report later proved to be false.

One person who breathed a sigh of relief was a Mr L Wells, who received a message telling of the sinking of *Titanic* while he was on his way from England to Australia aboard SS *Orsova* soon after the disaster. His sister and her husband had been booked to sail on the doomed ship, but they changed their mind at the last minute.

On 18 April a New York newspaper reported: 'The captain of the steamship *La Bretagne*, which has arrived here, reports that on the voyage across the Atlantic he saw huge icebergs. Forty polar bears were seen clinging to the surfaces of the giant bergs.'

A German ship named *Clio* reported sighting a broken iceberg 130ft high, carrying saloon fittings, chairs, hand-bags, cushions and wreckage believed to have formed part of *Titanic.*

On arriving in New York on 24 April, the officers of the North German Lloyd steamer *Princess Irene* stated:

> The wireless operator intercepted a despatch in which some ships reported, in passing a spot approximately 50 miles from the scene of Titanic disaster, that they had sighted an iceberg on which were the bodies of more than a dozen men wearing lifebelts. The opinion of the officers was that the men climbed on the mass of ice and had frozen to death. No attempt was made to take the bodies off.

The White Star Line contracted four vessels to search for bodies in the area of the sea where she sank. A cable-repair ship based at Halifax in Nova Scotia, Canada, called the CS *Mackay-Bennett* sailed from Halifax on 21 April and searched the disaster area a few days later.

Newspapers reported:

> A Gruesome Titanic Story. What the Funeral Ship Saw: The first man to land from the funeral ship which was sent out from New York to recover bodies was Mr John Snow, who superintended the work of embalming the dead, and generally directed the caring for the bodies as they were recovered from the ocean.
>
> 'Among the bodies recovered is that of a two-year-old baby boy. He came floating to us with upturned face. His was the only body

recovered which had no lifebelt. Nothing I have ever seen at sea made such an impression on me.

'We secured about 40 miles from the scene of the disaster the bodies of twelve women. It has been stated that there was an explosion in the sinking Titanic and this probably explains the terribly mutilated condition of many of the bodies. Arms and legs were shattered and faces and bodies mangled. We picked up many lifebelts 170 miles from the wreck.

'Many of the bodies were of persons in full evening dress. All the watches worn by the men had stopped at precisely ten minutes past 2. There was hardly any variation.

'We recovered in all 306 bodies, buried 116 at sea, and have brought home 190. There was evidence of a fierce struggle for life in some cases. Hands were clutching clothing, and faces were distorted with terror. Ours was a terrible task.

'There was a special service for each body buried at sea, the hymn, "Jesus, Lover of my Soul" being sung. We found and photographed the black iceberg which caused the wreck. It was an immense berg, but badly shattered.

'As soon as the ship was docked, Captain Richard Roberts, commander of Mr Astor's yacht, went on board, and a coffin was pulled away from a pile on the after deck, and opened. Mr Roberts looked in. "That is Colonel Astor." he said. The body was dressed in blue suit, and had been found encased in a life-belt, and floating in an upright position. Round the waist was a gold buckle, and in the pockets £500 in notes and cash.

'By far the greater number of the bodies recovered were floating in groups of 20 or more amid the debris. Buoyed up by their cork belts, the bodies at a distance looked like a flock of gulls at rest on the water. Like Mr Astor, they were all in an upright position, as if treading water.'

Most of the recovered victims were buried in two separate mass graves in Fairview Lawn Cemetery at Halifax, while others were claimed by their families from around the world and transported for repatriation.

The Western Union's CS *Minia* left Halifax on 22 April and because of bad weather it only recovered seventeen bodies, all apparently miles apart from each other. As the ship was searching the area where the disaster occurred. Captain William De Carteret took a picture of an iceberg and stated that a long red streak that could be clearly seen along its side indicated a possible collision with an ocean liner. However, the German ship SMS *Prinz Adalbert* had set sail on 15 April 1912, and *Titanic* disaster was still unknown to the members of its crew. Visibility was clear, and the chief steward of the liner, M Linoenewald, noticed a huge red streak on an iceberg, as if something had dragged against it, and the steward took a photograph of it. Could there have been two icebergs with red streaks, or was it the same iceberg. After studying both photographs, the two icebergs look different, and the CS *Minia* photograph matches the descriptions by the survivors of the disaster more accurately. Perhaps the red streak is some kind of natural phenomenon?

The *Montmagny* left Halifax on 6 May and picked up four bodies; and on 25 May an Irish saloon steward named James McGrady was the only body saved from the sea by the SS *Algernine*, after three weeks of searching.

RMS *Oceanic* found the 'collapsible A' lifeboat on 16 May, which contained the body of a Canadian businessman named Thomson Beattie, still wearing his dinner suit, and two firemen. He was buried at sea on his mother's birthday, in the area of the sea where she had been born on a ship bound for Canada.

On 17 May newspapers reported:

> The body of a fireman has been found in a boat by the Oceanic, chained by the leg to the thwart, and the bodies of two men were huddled together and had corks in their mouths. The Oceanic's doctor believes the men chewed them in their delirium to ease the pangs of hunger and thirst.

A bedroom steward from Dorset named William Thomas Kerly was picked up by the tanker SS *Ottawa* on 6 June, and fifty-four days after the disaster the last body was retrieved from the icy waters. It was clad in a life jacket, and had drifted 375 miles from the wreck site. It was that of first-class saloon steward William Frederick Cheverton, which was picked up by the SS *Ilford* on 8 June 1912, and was buried at sea. He was a Royal Navy veteran.

On the first anniversary of the disaster an Australian newspaper reported:

> Mr W F Bassett, chief officer on the steamer *Ilford*, which arrived at Newcastle yesterday from Moji, gave a representative of the *Newcastle Morning Herald* an interesting account of the discovery by him of the body of one of the victims of *Titanic* disaster. Yesterday was the anniversary of that awful calamity.
>
> On June 8 last year, when the *Ilford* was in latitude 46.06 north, longitude 42.51 west, bound from Galveston to Hamburg, Mr Bassett was on the bridge at about noon, when his attention was attracted by an object in the water. On using the glasses he saw that it was a body. The steamer was stopped and a boat lowered with Mr Bassett and the third officer and two seamen.
>
> On recovering the body it was found to be encircled by a lifebelt and from letters, postcards and Christmas cards found in the pockets of the clothing it was ascertained that it was that of W F Cheverton, a steward on the ill-fated *Titanic*. A Watch and chain, bunch if keys, knife and silver pencil case were also found, and these were handed over to the British Consul in Hamburg for despatch to the deceased's relatives in England, at the address shown in the letters.
>
> The body, after the removal of the articles mentioned from the pockets, was weighted and consigned to the deep. It had been in the water for 54 days, and carried by the Gulf stream at the rate of seven miles a day to where it was found.

On 10 June it was reported under the heading 'Floating Lifeboat: Mystery of the Sea':

> The German steamer *Essenbach*, while on her voyage to this port (Baltimore), sighted a barnacle-covered lifeboat near the scene of Titanic disaster. The master of the *Essenbach* did not deem it worth his while to examine the boat, so that it is unknown as to whether there were any bodies on board.

In mid-July 1931 it was reported from New York, 'After having washed about in the sea for 19 years, a lifebelt marked "SS Titanic" was washed up on the shore of Gravesend Bay, New York, recently'.

On 30 April 1912, the father of band member Jock Hume received an unsympathetic, now notorious, note from Blacks, which requested 'We shall be obliged if you will remit us the sum of 5s.4d, which is owing to us as per enclosed statement. We shall also be obliged if you will settle the enclosed uniform account.' The uniform account included items such as lyre lapel insignia and sewing White Star buttons on tunic, and the total bill was 14 shillings and 7 pence.

Under the heading 'Lost Fireman's Vindication', the *Southampton Times and Hampshire Express* stated:

> That there was a man named James Hart on *Titanic* there is no doubt. J Hart of 51 College Street, attached his signature to the ship's articles, and the inference was that he had sailed under false pretences. The suggestion that he used another man's book has given intense pain to the members of the family, who indignantly deny the statement.
>
> Mr Hart has sailed out of Southampton for over twenty years. He served the Union Castle Company and the RMSP before transferring to the White Star Line, and we are assured that his discharge book was a good one. There was, therefore, no reason why he should hide behind another man's character, and that he made no attempt to do so is proved by the fact that he gave his College Street address when signing on. Had he assumed the name of the Liverpool man, he must also have given the Liverpool address of that fireman. J Hart was a member of the British Seafarers' Union, and we have been asked by the members of his family to publish these facts in order that the dead man might be vindicated.

On 9 May 1912 The Apollo Club in Brooklyn, New York, held a concert to raise funds to help the families of the musicians who perished on *Titanic.* However, the most impressive memorial of all took part in early July when there was a 'Great Memorial Concert' held at the Royal Albert Hall in memory of *Titanic* musicians. Newspapers reported:

> Under the auspices of the Orchestral Association of England a great memorial concert was given in the Royal Albert Hall, London, on Friday, May 24 last (Empire Day) in honour of Titanic bandsmen who perished on Titanic on April 15 last. A copy of the programme has been received from London by Mr James Booth. The orchestra

The Royal Mail ships *Titanic* and *Olympic* under construction at the Harland and Wolf shipyard. The *Olympic* was launched first, and after it was involved in a collision with HMS *Hawke* they had to pull resources from *Titanic,* which fatefully delayed her maiden voyage from 20 March to 10 April.

The first class smoke room was one of the grandest areas on *Titanic*. It was decorated with intricately-carved dark mahogany wood, which was inlaid with mother of pearl patterns, red and blue lino tiles, and stained glass windows. The interior windows were illuminated by electric light.

The ship's main feature was the Grand Staircase. It was built from English solid oak, and enhanced with wrought iron. The decorated glass domes above were designed to let in as much natural light as possible.

Five tug boats guide *Titanic* out of Belfast harbour for sea trials.

Titanic leaves berth 43 at Dock Gate 4, the entrance to the Eastern Dock in Southampton, to begin its fateful voyage across the Atlantic Ocean; a journey from which it never returned.

Tom Andrews seated next to his mother with his family. His father and brothers rose to high office in Irish politics and administration. He was in his 40th year when he went down with the ship he had been prominent in designing.

Captain Edward Smith was a native of Stoke-on-Trent, with 32 years of service with the White Star Line. He was considering retirement when he lost his life in the *Titanic* disaster.

Charles Lightoller, known as 'Lights', went to sea at the age of 13. He was the second officer aboard *Titanic*, and played a prominent part in the evacuation of the ship. A veteran of the Dunkirk evacuation, he saw service in the two World Wars, being awarded the Distinguished Service Cross and bar.

Harold Bride (on the right of picture) was a Marconi wireless operator on several ships before being appointed junior officer on *Titanic*. He gave evidence at the enquiry concerning the disaster, but he was involved in a serious incident during the evacuation for which he later decided he preferred not to talk about.

Alfred Allsop was keen on learning about the power of electricity at an early age. He and his team kept the lights working on the ship for as long as they could so the passengers could locate the lifeboats right until it went down – taking all the electricians with it.

Wallace Hartley and his band were given the responsibility of providing music on the ship. They played their instruments for as long as they could to try to keep spirits up. All eight musicians lost their lives in the disaster.

Violet Jessop in her British Red Cross nurses uniform during the Great War. She was one of a few people who worked on all three White Star liners, and was therefore involved in three shipping disasters.

Tom Whiteley left a detailed account of his ordeal in the *Titanic* disaster, during which he suffered a broken leg and frostbite.

James Hart was serving as a fireman when he lost his life in the *Titanic* disaster. His initial of J on his recruitment papers was mistaken for a T, and Thomas Hart was recorded as being the man who had died. However, this man had lost his signing-on papers and did not sail, causing a shock to his mother when he returned to his home in Liverpool. In James Cameron's film an infamous game of cards (or chance) took place in which Leonardo DiCaprio gambled with his ship's papers. This scene is based on the Thomas Hart incident.

James Witter from Ormskirk in Lancashire was a smoke room steward. He survived the sinking, but he rarely spoke of the disaster, and was said to have been haunted by it for the rest of his life.

Joseph Hyman was a Russian Jew based in Manchester. On his return he set-up a small delicatessen in the city, which came to be known locally as 'Titanic's', and is still trading.

Algie Barkworth was born at Tranby House near Hull, and lived there for most of his life. He survived the sinking, and died unmarried at the age of 80.

Joseph Fynney owned a firm of rubber manufacturers in Liverpool. He was known to have enjoyed the company of young men, and was travelling with a teenager named Alfred Gaskell. They both died in the disaster, and Joe's body was not recovered from the sea until nearly three weeks later.

Adolph Saalfeld was of German descent. He was travelling to America to present a selection of perfumes which he carried in 65 little glass bottles. Adolph survived the disaster but his precious bottles went down with the ship. Miraculously, all but three of them were recovered from the sea bed in 2000.

Alice Phillips was a West Country girl travelling with her father, who became a victim of the sinking. Alice later married and had a daughter. She died in Salford in 1923, the victim of a flu epidemic.

Michel and Edmond Navratil were travelling with their father, Michel, who had taken them away from their mother without her knowledge of his actions. Michel senior was lost in the sinking but the two children survived. They had been known only as Lolo and Momon, and their mother only discovered their whereabouts after reading about the two 'Titanic Orphans'.

Young Eva Hart enjoyed singing and she was due to perform in a concert on the night of the disaster. Her mother Esther survived but her father did not.

The story of the life of Kate Phillips is one of the most tragic in connection with the *Titanic* disaster. Kate had been eloping with her employer, Henry Morley, when he went down with the ship. The experience disturbed her mind, and she had been admitted to an asylum at one point in her life.
A pendant known as 'Love of the Sea' that Henry had given to Kate during the voyage, is believed to have been the inspiration for the 'Heart of the Ocean' storyline between Rose (Kate Winslet) and Jack (Leonardo DiCaprio) in James Cameron's film.

The reason why some of the passengers refused to leave *Titanic* is understandable. To them the choice was to remain aboard in what they thought was the comparative safety of a large ship that was designed to take on water and not sink, and wait until the problem was fixed or help came; or go out into the cold dark night on a small overcrowded lifeboat, with no heat or light and uncomfortable seating, to be sprayed by freezing water.

Men who manned the lifeboats rowed with all their strength to try to get away from the stricken ship for fear that they might get sucked down with it as it sank.

The CS *Carpathia* was on its way from New York to Gibraltar and fortunately was in the region. On receiving a distress signal from *Titanic* it immediately set a course towards the disaster area. After working through dangerous ice fields it arrived at the scene of devastation at four o'clock in the morning of 15 April.

A Titanic lifeboat with its survivors drifting in choppy waters as it approached *Carpathia*.

Lifeboat 14 and collapsible D reach *Carpathia*. Lifeboat 14 was under the command of Harold Lowe, with Joe Scarrott assisting. Among the passengers were Clear Cameron and Nellie Wallcroft, and Emily and Eva Hart. The two Navratil boys and a dog were among the survivors in Collapsible D.

Some survivors pictured aboard *Carpathia*. Passengers and crew on the rescue ship provided them with warm clothing, and some even gave up their cabins to be used by *Titanic* victims.

Harold Bride's desperate experiences during the disaster left him with a sprained ankle and frostbite, and he had to be assisted off *Carpathia* on its arrival in New York.

On 22 April 1914, 100,000 people packed into East Andrews Park in Southampton for the unveiling of a bronze and granite Titanic Engineers Memorial. It was renovated in 2010.

The bronze bust of *Titanic* bandleader, Wallace Hartley, which was erected at his home town of Colne in Lancashire in 1915.

> was composed of 100 instrumentalists, chosen from seven of the leading orchestras of London. The conductors were Sir Edward Elgar (London Symphony Orchestra), Sir Henry J Wood (Queen's Hall Orchestra), Mr Landon Ronald (New Symphony Orchestra), Mr Thomas Beecham (Beecham Symphony Orchestra), Mr Percy Pitt (Musical Director of the Royal Opera House), M Fritz Ernaldy (London Opera House), and Herr Mengelberg, each of whom led the musicians in chosen numbers. Among the compositions played were Chopin's *Funeral March* and *Nearer, My God, to Thee.* Madame Ada Crossley, the famous Australian singer, also contributed to the programme.

Some newspapers reported 'It is stated that M Glazounoff, the Russian composer, is composing a symphony for orchestra and chorus on the subject of *Titanic* disaster to be called 'The Song of Death', the whole voyage of the ill-fated vessel being depicted.' However, it seems that this project never materialised.

During the passage of the steamer *Franconia* across the Atlantic a year after the disaster, it sailed into the vicinity of the spot where *Titanic* went down. Laurel wreaths were cast into the sea and the crew of 1,300 men and women stood on the deck with bowed heads, while the ship's band played the hymn *Nearer, My God, to Thee.*

Mysteries and legends concerning *Titanic* disaster and its victims began to be reported soon afterwards. On 23 July 1912 a Baltimore newspaper reported:

> 'Titanic Mystery' – 'Captain Smith said to be in Hiding' – Peter Pryall, veteran captain of Montreal, and a life-long friend of Captain Smith, of *Titanic*, swears that Captain Smith was not drowned. Pryall declares that he saw him recently in Baltimore. Captain Smith tried to evade him by taking the train bound for Washington. It is stated that Captain Smith's nephew, a resident of Baltimore, disappeared the day after his uncle's re-appearance.

One of the victims of the disaster was the well-known spiritualist of the time, William Thomas Stead, who had been reported to have been sat in the first-class smoking room patiently reading a book as the tragic events unfolded all around him, as if his death was inevitable to him. Newspapers in early November 1913 reported under the headings:

'From the Other World; W T Stead Appears to a Friend: Explains His Sensations':

> General, Sir Alfred Turner KCB, will tell for the first time in a book now on the eve of publication the connected story of Mr W T Stead's appearance to him at his residence, Carlyle House, Chelsea Embankment.
>
> 'The first manifestation of Mr Stead, within a week of Titanic disaster, occurred in this very room. Probably the first manifestation was a shadow seen on a glass, but I am speaking now of the audible voice on an occasion subsequently.
>
> 'I went to Cambridge House in Wimbledon, Mr Stead's home, and there, at a miscellaneous circle … Mr Stead appeared twice, at my right shoulder. The appearances were short and transient, not exactly flashes – more than that – but they rapidly faded. But the voice was very well heard.'
>
> 'And what did the voice say, Sir Alfred?'
>
> '"I am very happy to be with you again." was the first words of greeting.'
>
> '"When *Titanic* sank, there was for myself a very short, sharp struggle to regain breath, and I came to my senses – it seemed in an instant – surrounded by hundreds of beings who, like myself, had passed over to a new existence, but were utterly unable to realise what had happened. They were quite unconscious of the fact that they were not still in the flesh. They were groping about in obscurity and uncertainty, and I set myself at once to do missionary work by enlightening the people as to what had happened and what was their new condition."'

As a point of interest it has been reported:

> 'It was Mr Stead who revealed the fact that the hymn *Nearer, My God, to Thee* was a favourite with King Edward. Mr Stead had hit upon the idea of publishing a work *Hymns That Have Helped*, and it contained *Nearer, My God, to Thee*, and there was a note attached that the then Prince of Wales had been appealed to for an opinion as to a hymn which had helped him most. Mr Stead received a reply from the Prince to the effect that while he had not made a special study of hymns, the one *Nearer, My God, to Thee* had interest to him.'

In January 1913, under the headings: 'Italian National Lottery Winner' and 'Fortune Waiting' several newspapers reported that 'The authorities are unable to trace the winner of a £60,000 prize in the national lottery. It is believed the winner was lost in *Titanic* disaster.'

Jeremiah Burke and Hanora Hegarty were lost in the disaster. In the early summer of 1913 a man was walking his dog along a shingle beach near Cork Harbour when he found the bottle that Jeremiah had thrown off *Titanic* as it departed Queenstown. The date on the note looks like a 10 to this writer, and it is certainly not a 15. However, it has been suggested that the date is a 13 and that the note was thrown from *Titanic* as it sank and drifted all the way back to Ireland.

In early 1928, Mrs E Robertson telephoned the local newspaper at Coalville in Leicestershire enquiring if her mother was still alive. Mrs Robertson had left home to board *Titanic* but had cancelled her booked passage on the ill-fated liner at the last minute. She told nobody of her intentions and therefore her family thought she had gone down with the ship. The local newspaper located her mother, who agreed to see her, and one of her daughters met her at the train station. She stated that during the Great War she had been doing war work and that she had been captured by the Germans. She stayed in Coalville for two nights and on leaving she gave no indication of her future plans.

While the American Senate enquiry into the disaster was being conducted in late April 1912, the following article appeared in several newspapers under the heading 'Titanic Disaster':

> As time proceeds further light is being thrown upon the wreck of the *Titanic*; but there is much that is still obscure and confusing. The committee appointed by the American Senate is continuing its inquiry, and the fourth officer of the ill-fated vessel has made a grave allegation to the effect that a mysterious ship was seen at the time of the disaster, only five miles away, but that she passed without acknowledging Titanic's signals of distress.
>
> Full inquiry into the calamity has been promised by Mr Sydney Buxton, President of the British Board of Trade. The New York correspondent of the *London Daily News* states that the Senate intends inquiring as to:
>
> 1. Whether the officers of the *Titanic* disregarded repeated warnings of the presence of icebergs?

2. Whether it was unavoidable that 100 women should have perished?
3. Why the White Star company was ignorant of the disaster until Monday evening, though both the *Baltic* and the *Olympic* knew details at noon?
4. Why a Marconi company's official sent a wireless to the operator on the *Carpathia* on Thursday: 'Say nothing. Hold your story for dollars in four figures.'

Lord Mersey presided over the British Wreck Commissioner's enquiry on behalf of the British Board of Trade, which took place in London from 2 May to 3 July 1912, but none of these questions were answered conclusively.

A Titanic Fund was set up to support the survivors and their families, which at one time reached nearly £2 million in today's money. It was wound up in 1959, with the balance transferred into annuities or the Shipwrecked Fishermen and Mariner's Royal Benevolent Society.

The third ship in the Olympic Class was RMS *Britannic,* which was launched on 26 February 1914. On the outbreak of the Great War it was commissioned as a hospital ship serving between the United Kingdom and the Dardanelles. The ship was sailing across the Aegean Sea on the morning of 21 November 1916 when it hit an enemy mine. It sank in less than an hour, and thirty people lost their lives. Aboard were Nurse Violet Jessop and Fireman John Priest, who became famous as 'The Unsinkable', having then survived disasters on all three of the White Star Line's Olympic-class liners. John Priest's brother Harry was also on the *Britannic*, and John also survived when the SS *Donegal* was torpedoed and sank on 17 April 1917. He claimed that he had to give up the sea because in the end nobody would sail with him. HMHS *Britannic* is the largest passenger ship on the sea floor, and was explored by Jacques Cousteau in 1975.

On 15 May 1934, RMS *Olympic* struck and sank the lightship *Nantucket* as it entered New York harbour, causing the deaths of four people. Soon afterwards, White Star merged with Cunard and when the *Queen Mary* and the *Queen Elizabeth* were built, they took over the company's express service and the old ships were gradually retired. *Olympic* was laid up and scrapped in 1935.

The legacy of *Titanic* also lives on through the many impressive memorials and monuments set up to commemorate the ship and its victims. The Liverpool Titanic and Engineers memorial was erected soon after the disaster, and the

Glasgow Institute of Marine Engineers memorial, as well as the Institute of Marine Engineers memorial in London. The Southampton Engineers Memorial in East Park was erected in 1914, and is perhaps the most famous of all the memorials dedicated to those who were on the ship when it floundered.

In 1932 the BBC announced that it was to broadcast a play based on the sinking of *Titanic*. The captain of the rescue ship, Sir Arthur Rostron, protested against it, saying:

> The Corporation should think of the feelings of the relatives of the drowned and of the remainder of the 700 survivors who are still alive. It would be too cruel for anyone intimately concerned with the tragedy to be drawn into re-living the catastrophe. Some of the scenes during the rescue of the passengers will haunt me forever. I shall not listen.

Arthur was a native of Bolton. After *Carpathia* he took over charge of the *Mauretania* from 1915 to 1926. He was awarded the Congressional Medal of Honour in 1913, and he was knighted in 1926; the same year he was granted the Freedom of the City of New York. From 1928 to 1931 he was commodore of the Cunard fleet. He died in 1940.

A children's book was published in 2011 by Nicola Pierce entitled *Spirit of Titanic*, in which a fictionalised version of Samuel Scott haunts the ship and observes its ill-fated voyage. It generated interest in Samuel's tragic story and later in the year a memorial stone was placed at his previously unmarked grave. During the centenary year of the disaster a plaque was unveiled at the Harland and Wolff Welders Club in east Belfast to commemorate the eight men who lost their lives during the construction of the vessel.

Titanic Belfast attraction opened on the actual site where *Titanic* was built, and a plaque dedicated to all the passengers and crew was unveiled at Dock Gate 4 on 10 April 1993, which is where *Titanic* was moored before setting out on its fateful voyage.

Millvina Dean, who was the baby in arms rescued in lifeboat 14, became the last-known survivor of the disaster when she died in 2009, aged 97.

During one of her many interviews, Eva Hart stated:

> It is not because it was the largest and most luxurious ship in the world. Quite simply, it is because Titanic is the one and only

> disaster – land, sea and air – for which there was no excuse for anyone to die.
>
> It was the murder of 1516 people who had to die because there were not any lifeboats ... a dreadful waste of life.

After numerous failed attempts to find the wreck of *Titanic*, in 1985 Robert Ballard led a Franco-American expedition over 12,000ft to the bottom of the Atlantic Ocean off the coast of Newfoundland, and on 1 September of that year they located the ship in what is now known as Titanic Canyon. The two sections were about a third of a mile apart.

In 2012 some 5,500 items from *Titanic* came up for sale in the United States. The items ranged from jewels and fine china to a 15-tonne portion of the hull. In 2007 the collection was valued at $189 million.

The last expedition to the wreck of the RMS *Titanic* to date was undertaken in early August 2019, under the command of Victor Vescovo of the Caladan Oceanic Company. A team of divers made five visits to the wreck and were able to take good-quality 4k images. However, it was also discovered that natural deterioration caused by metal-eating bacteria, corrosion and the ocean's strong currents was causing deterioration of the structure of the ship. In particular the divers discovered the partial collapse of the hull near the officers' quarters on the starboard side, causing the deterioration of the staterooms, and the 'captain's bath tub', which has been a fond image among *Titanic* enthusiasts, is no longer visible.

Titanic disaster has also been the inspiration for works of both fiction and non-fiction. The first film ever released was named *Saved from Titanic*, which was an American silent movie depicting the disaster, which came out only twenty-nine days after the ship went down, and casting Dorothy Gibson, an actual survivor, in its star role. James Cameron released his *Titanic* in 1997, which won eleven Academy Awards (including best picture) and is still extremely popular today.

Titanic: The Musical opened on Broadway in 1997. It was originally met with scepticism as a musical about the most tragic disaster in maritime history hardly seemed fitting. However, it deals with the people in a respectful way and went on to win five Tony Awards, including Best Musical. It made its first tour of the United Kingdom in 2018.

PART II

Biographical tributes to most of the people who appear in the main text

Alfred Samuel Allsop

Fred Allsop was born during the second half of 1876 at 96 Brunswick Street, Chorlton-on-Medlock, Manchester. He was the youngest of four sons in a family of thirteen children to George Foster Allsop (born at Chorlton-on-Medlock in 1833), a travelling salesman, and his wife, Elizabeth (formerly Walker), who was the daughter of a teacher, born in County Tyrone, Ireland in 1837 (died in 1917). They may have met in Melbourne, Australia, and had two children while they were there: Ada Ellen was born at Singleton in Melbourne, New South Wales, Australia, on 23 April 1856; and Henry Edward was born at Singleton in 1858. On their return to England, they married in 1860 at Manchester Cathedral, where most of their children were christened. One of Alfred's sisters had died before he was born.

By the time of the 1891 census they had moved to 29 Broughton Lane in the district of Lower Broughton, Salford, and Alfred became well known for his interest in the power of electricity at an early age, spending much of his time riding on the electric tram cars in Manchester. He was a regular visitor at the Salford power station in Bloom Street, which supplied the bulk of traction supply for central Manchester, plus lighting and power demand.

His father died in Salford on 29 November 1896, and the family moved to a house called Mountpellier on Marine Parade in Great Clacton, Essex; although Alfred was described as an electrical engineer living at Rosslyn Park in the Toxteth district of Liverpool.

When he was fifteen he began an apprenticeship with H H Hall and Company of Liverpool, which was pioneering the use of ships telephones, followed by employment with Campbell and Isherwood of Bootle, where he worked in the development of electrical switchboards. This was followed by short spells at the Hame Electric Company and the Northern Electric Company, both of Liverpool.

He took up an appointment on the *Baltic*, and joined the White Star Line in August 1904 as assistant electrician aboard the *Celtic II*. He later served on the *Majestic* and *Oceanic*, in which it is said he crossed the Atlantic about a hundred times before joining *Titanic*.

On 17 October 1908, at All Saints Church in Princes Park, Liverpool, he married Hilda Barnes, who had been born at Ashbourne in Derbyshire in 1886, and was the daughter of Thomas John Barnes and his wife, Helena. When the White Star Line moved their headquarters to Southampton, Alfred and Hilda also moved to that town. Their only child, Philip Alfred, was born at Southampton in 2 February 1911. In the census that soon followed Alfred was at sea, but Hilda and Philip were recorded as visitors at 15 Suffolk Avenue in Shirley, Southampton.

Alfred was one of the transfer crew that brought *Titanic* to Southampton on 2 April, where he signed on as second electrician a few days later, and he gave his address as 134 Malmesbury Road in Freemantle, Southampton.

There were six electrical engineers in *Titanic*'s crew, their working clothes usually being a uniform jacket over a brown boiler suit. Alfred was known as the junior or second electrician, and the other four were assistant electricians. The level of responsibility may be gauged by the pay scales: the chief would have received £12 for the voyage, Alfred received £11, and the assistants received £8 each. Alfred's pay was higher than that of the chief surgeon or of any of the deck crew below the rank of second officer. Among the engineers in general the ranking system can be confusing, and 'juniors' were often quite senior! The junior assistant second engineer was several ranks senior to the senior fifth engineer.

Alfred lost his life in the disaster and his body was never recovered. His estate was administered to his widow, and Hilda also benefitted from Titanic Relief Fund 'for expenses due to the illness of her little boy'.

Alfred is named on the Liverpool Titanic and Engineers memorial, and he is named on the Southampton Engineers Memorial in East Park, on the Glasgow Institute of Marine Engineers memorial, and on the Institute of Marine Engineers memorial in London.

Charles Edward Andrews

Charles Andrews was born at West Derby in Liverpool on 18 January 1893, the third of five sons in the family of eight children born between 1881 and 1898 to Henry Jeremiah Andrews (born in 1857), and his wife, Emily Anne (formerly Robertson, 1859-1920), who had married in their native town of Southampton in 1879. Henry was a seaman, and it was his work that took him north to Liverpool.

The 1891 census records him as living with his family at a house called 'Oakleigh' on Bedford Road in the district of Walton-on-the-Hill in Liverpool, but two decades later they had moved back south to 145 Millbrook Road in the district of Freemantle, Southampton.

Charles reportedly went to sea at the age of fifteen, so therefore he was absent from the 1911 census. He was a keen swimmer, for which he is reported to have gained several awards.

He was on board *Olympic* when it collided with HMS *Hawke*, and he had been with the White Star Line for four years, having previously served on *Oceanic*. He was aged nineteen when he signed on to *Titanic* as an assistant officer's saloon steward, on 10 April 1912. His cousin, George Robertson, also signed on as a steward. He was rescued in lifeboat 16, and he later testified at the Senate Inquiry into the sinking.

He signed on to *Oceanic* again on 10 July 1912, and he continued working at sea through the two world wars. He later served on the *Aquitania* as a steward and then on the *Queen Mary* as a masseur and swimming pool attendant. He then served on the *Queen Elizabeth* until his retirement in 1959.

In 1932 he married Ivy Winifred Powell, at Millbrook Church in Southampton. She had been born on 1 January 1903, at Eling in Totton, Hampshire. They had children named Ann Marina, born in 1934, and Edward, born in 1937.

Charles died on 2 January 1961, aged sixty-seven, and his ashes were scattered in the South Stoneham Cemetery in Swaythling, Southampton. His wife died in 1979.

Thomas Andrews

Thomas Andrews, who became known as Tommie, was born into a prominent administrative Ulster family on 7 February 1873, at Ardara House in Comber near Newtownards, County Down, Ireland. The house is now flats, which include a Titanic Suite. He was the second son of the Right Honourable Thomas Andrews (1843-1916), a member of the Privy Council of Ireland, and his wife, Eliza (formerly Pirrie, 1845-1929). His older brother was John Miller Andrews, who was Prime Minister of Northern Ireland from 1940 to 1943, and his younger brother was Sir James Andrews, who was

Lord Chief Justice of Northern Ireland from 1937 to 1951. He was a nephew of Lord William James Pirrie, the principal owner of the Harland and Wolff Company in Belfast.

He has been described as 'A healthy, energetic, bonny child, and grew into a handsome, plucky and lovable boy'. Like his father and other members of the family, he was educated at the Royal Belfast Academical Institution from 1884, and in 1889, aged just 16, he gained employment at the Harland and Wolff Shipyard as an apprentice. He was under the guidance of his uncle, however, it is recorded that he showed great aptitude and industry, and during this time he studied in the evenings.

After the completion of his apprenticeship, his promotion was rapid and entirely due to his own ability and energy. He became very popular, and he was appointed as one of the outside managers in the shipyard. In 1894 he was given charge of the repair department, in which capacity his abilities were thoroughly tested as some of the most difficult engineering achievements were supervised by him at a very young age. He was involved in the repair and construction of numerous vessels, including the *Baltic* and the *Oceanic*. He was noted as a hardworking man and for his innovative designs, and he became the manager of the design department.

Among his memberships of several influential institutions, he became a member of the Royal Institution of Naval Architects in 1901, and the Institution of Mechanical Engineers in 1902.

In 1907 he was appointed a managing director at Harland and Wolff. In the same year the White Star Line decided to create a class of luxury liners and the project was given to the Belfast shipyard. Consequently, Thomas became the main architect of both the *Olympic* and *Titanic*.

On 24 June 1908 he married Helen Reilly Barbour (born at Warwick on 10 April 1881). She was the daughter of the textile industrialist John Doherty Barbour. They made their home at a house called Dunallan at 20 Windsor Avenue in Belfast. On 27 November 1910, they had a daughter named Elizabeth Law Barbour Andrews, who was usually known by her initials of ELBA. She became the first woman ever to receive a pilot's licence in Northern Ireland.

On his untimely death, the Institution of Mechanical Engineers stated: 'His knowledge of naval architecture embraced electrical and mechanical engineering as well as marine engineering, his experience of all the complicated and intricate machinery and arrangements necessary in the construction and equipment of modern steam ships being altogether exceptional.'

His wife received the following letter from Bruce Ismay:

> Forgive me for intruding upon your grief, but I feel I must send you a line to convey my most deep and sincere sympathy with you in the terrible loss you have suffered. It is impossible for me to express in words all I feel, or make you realise how truly sorry I am for you, or how my heart goes out to you. I knew your husband for many years, and had the highest regard for him, and looked upon him as a true friend. No one who had the pleasure of knowing him could fail to realise and appreciate his numerous good qualities and he will be sadly missed in his profession. Nobody did more for the White Star Line, or was more loyal to its interests than your good husband, and I always placed the utmost reliance on his judgment.
>
> If we miss him and feel his loss so keenly, what your feelings must be I cannot think. Words at such a time are useless, but I could not help writing to you to tell you how truly deeply I feel for you in your grief and sorrow.

On 8 February 1917, Helen married Henry Peirson Harland, a member of the family of the owners of the shipyard. She died in Northern Ireland on 22 August 1966, aged eighty-five. Elizabeth never married and was killed in a traffic accident in County Dublin, Ireland on 1 November 1973. There are no living descendants of Thomas Andrews, but his wife had four children with her second husband and there are living descendants of that lineage.

The SS *Nomadic*, the only ship designed by Tommie that still survives, remains on display in Belfast in his honour.

Thomas was in his fortieth year at the time of his death, and in James Cameron's 1997 film *Titanic* he was portrayed by Victor Garber, a forty-eight-year-old Canadian.

Algernon Henry (Wilson) Barkworth

Algernon 'Algy' Barkworth was born at Tranby House in Heads Lane, Hessle near Kingston upon Hull in East Yorkshire, on 4 June 1864. He was the second of three sons in the family of five children of Henry Boulderston Barkworth (born at Tranby House on 15 January 1822, died at Tranby

House on his seventy-sixth birthday, 15 January 1898), and Catherine Hester (formerly Smith, born in India in 1838). His father was a timber merchant, farmer and landowner. Algy was educated at Eton College.

The house was originally built in 1807, by John Barkworth, a merchant who made his fortune in the shipping industry, and it was passed down the generations to Algernon, who was his great-nephew. Algernon grew up surrounded by an entourage of servants and maids, and he was mainly raised by his governess, Amelia Selina Coxhead (1844-1920).

In 1903 Algernon was appointed a Justice of the Peace for the East Riding of Yorkshire, and during the early part of the twentieth century he lived next door to his brother, Edmund, who was a farmer and landowner in Puddletrenthide, a village in Dorset. In about 1911 he decided to return to Tranby House to live with his widowed mother and unmarried sister, Evelyn.

Algie survived the sinking, and before he returned to England he spent a short time at the home of Mrs Richard F Wood in Concord, Massachusetts. His hands were so frozen that he had to dictate his account to a Mrs Francis, who wrote it on the medical stationary of a Doctor Blackmarr. On 13 April he had sent a Marconigram to his mother in Scarborough that stated 'All well, Algy'. However, his family could not be sure if the message had been sent before or after the disaster, until they received a second message dated 18 April that reassured them by declaring 'Am safe on board *Carpathia* – Algy'. On 22 April a report appeared in the local newspaper that stated 'Please announce Algernon Barkworth, Hessle, arrived New York on *Carpathia*, ex *Titanic* sank. Jumped into sea, drop thirty feet. Just before she sank. Swam clear, and saw *Titanic* sink. Cold intense. Held onto overturned lifeboat for six hours. Picked up eventually by one of *Titanic's* boats. Suffering from frost-bitten fingers.' Two days later the Hessle Urban Council congratulated Mrs Barkworth on her son's survival.

Algy lived at Tranby House for the rest of his life and remained unmarried. Described as an eccentric, he loved animals and was a keen collector of curios. He was described as 'a gentleman if ever there was one – a type which is fast dying out'. He was appointed to the East Riding Bench in the month following the disaster, and retained the appointment until one year before his death. His family stated that he never married 'because he was not of that persuasion'.

After his mother's death on 29 August 1915, he and Evelyn continued to live in Tranby House, until her death on 29 April 1933. Towards the end of his life he suffered badly from respiratory problems, and he died on 7 January 1945, aged eighty. He was buried with his sister in Mill Lane Cemetery at Kirk Ella in Yorkshire.

Tranby House was bequeathed to the local education authority. It became Tranby High School in 1947, and is now known as Hessle High School. It became a Grade II listed building 1967, to ensure its history and architecture is protected.

George Barlow

George Barlow was born in Salford, on 4 May 1872, and was baptised on 17 July later that year. He was the son of George Barlow, who was a railway clerk, and his wife, Harriett (formerly Cooper). Both of his parents were born in Manchester in 1851, and they were married in 1871. George junior had an older sister named Lily Elizabeth, who was born with the surname of Cooper in 1870, and Annie was born in 1874.

Harriett died in 1876, aged only twenty-five, and George senior was remarried in the following year, to Emily Jane Cropley (1849-1941) of Spalding in Lincolnshire. Therefore George had a number of half-siblings born between 1879 and 1895.

In 1881 the family were living at 85 Moulton Street in Hulme, Manchester, and a decade later at 112 Wardle Street in Hulme, when George was described as a packer of cotton goods. By 1901 he was living with his sister, Lily (then Mrs Charles Hedley), at 36 Glebe Street in south Manchester, when he was still a packer. He was not recorded on the 1911 census, but his father and stepmother lived at 212 Raby Street in Moss Side, and George senior was still a railway clerk.

George signed on *Titanic* on 4 April 1912, as a second-class bedroom steward. The place recorded for his port of engagement is Carminster, which is on Foundry Lane in Southampton.

George Barlow lost his life in the disaster, and if his body was recovered it was never identified.

For several years after his death his family placed memorials in the *Manchester Evening News*. Those for 16 April 1917, read:

> BARLOW – In ever loving memory of our dear son, GEORGE, who lost his life on *Titanic*, April 15th, 1912. Dearly loved beyond words.

'Beneath the roll of soundless waves
Our best and loved one lies;
Give us to feel his spirit lives
Immortal in the skies.'
Father, Mother, Jessie, Florrie.

BARLOW – In loving memory of our dear friend, GEORGE,
who went down in Titanic, April 15th, 1912.
'Asleep in the deep.
God rest the great Titanic's noble dead.'
Agnes and Dick (in France)

Frederick Barrett

Fred Barrett was born at Bootle in Liverpool, on 10 January 1883, and was baptised at St John's Church in Bootle later that year. He was the only surviving child of Henry Charles Barrett, a timber labourer who was born in Devon in 1862, and his wife, Mary (formerly Morgan, born in Birkenhead in 1864). At the time of his birth the family home was at 14 Howe Street in Bootle, but by 1891 they were living at 16 Molyneux Street in Bootle, and Fred was described as a carman. His father appears to have died in 1909.

He is known to have worked as a fireman aboard RMS *Campania* in 1903, giving his address as 69 Lyon Street. He moved to the White Star Line, and during 1904 he worked on the *Parisian* and *Cedric*, returning to *Campania* in 1906. He had been working on *New York*, and was living at 24 King Street in Southampton, when he signed on *Titanic* on 6 April 1912. As a leading fireman he could expect wages of £6 10s a month. He was one of two men with the exact same name working as a fireman on the ship.

Fred was called to testify at both the American and British enquiries. On 25 May 1912, Fred was working on *Olympic* when Senator Smith was given a tour of her as part of his investigation. The captain mentioned that one of his stokers had been aboard *Titanic*, and the Senator went down to the engine room to talk with Fred and get a better impression of how conditions had been aboard *Titanic* in the boiler rooms at the time of the collision.

The *Daily Sketch* reported:

> Lord Mersey yesterday put a striking question to Frederick Barrett, a leading stoker on Titanic. After Barrett had described

> the outbreak of fire in one of the coal bunkers, Lord Mersey asked if he thought the Fire had anything to do with the disaster. Barrett replied that it would be hard to say. On the previous day Barrett was asked whether the rush of water that drove him on deck was due to a bulkhead giving way, but he said he could not say. Yesterday he said that after the bunker where the fire occurred had been cleared the bulkhead that ran by that bunker was damaged, and he attributed that to the fire.

On 16 February 1915, at St Nicholas Church in Liverpool, he married Mary Ann (born in 1882), the daughter of a carter named Thomas Jones. They both gave their address as Robert Street. Their one surviving child was named Harold, who was born in 1921.

Unfortunately, Mary Ann died in 1923, and he did not remarry. He worked as a timber labourer in Liverpool, giving his address as 22 Brasenose Road. He became afflicted with pulmonary tuberculosis and he died on 3 March 1931. His death left Harold as an orphan, who was raised by an uncle in Bootle.

Joseph William Bell

Joe Bell was born at Farlam House in Brampton, Cumberland (now Cumbria), on 12 March 1861, the oldest of three boys and a girl born between 1861 and 1869, to John Bell and his wife Margaret (formerly Watson). His parents and descendants were yeoman farmers at Farlam, and John Bell had inherited their farm from his father in 1849. There are memorials to the family at Farlam Churchyard, where Joseph was baptised on 4 May 1861. John moved the family to Stanwix, near Edentown, Carlisle, where Joseph went to the grammar school. John was a member of the Westmoreland and Cumberland Yeomanry Cavalry for over forty years, being latterly Quartermaster. He subsequently lived for many years in retirement at Bishopstown.

Joe served an apprenticeship at the famous Robert Stephenson Works at Newcastle upon Tyne, and commenced his seagoing career in 1883 with the Lamport and Holt Line of Liverpool. He joined the White Star line in 1885, and served on many vessels trading on the company`s New Zealand and New York services. At the age of thirty he was promoted to chief engineer on *Coptic* and he served aboard *Olympic* before being transferred to *Titanic*. He 'stood-by' the ship during her construction in Belfast.

He married Maud Bates at Ripley in 1893 and they had two boys and two girls between 1896 and 1908. His eldest boy, Frank, had recently left the Grosvenor Boarding School in Carlisle, and commenced an apprenticeship at Harland and Wolff, and accompanied his father aboard *Titanic* when the ship sailed from Belfast to Southampton. A member of the Institute of Marine Engineers, and of the Royal Naval Reserve, Joe lived at 1 Belvidere Road in Great Crosby, Liverpool, but had a temporary address in Southampton.

Joe Bell was in his fifty-first year when he died in the disaster and his body probably went down with the ship. He left a widow, Maud, with two boys and two girls. He is commemorated on his mother's grave memorial at Farlam Church, on the plaque in the old White Star building in Liverpool, and on a brass plaque at St Faith's Church in Crosby, Liverpool.

He was portrayed in the 1997 film *Titanic* by Terry Forrestal from Derbyshire. Terry was just under the age of fifty at the time of the film and he lost his life during a BASE jumping accident at the age of fifty-two.

Elizabeth 'Lily' Bonnell

Lily Bonnell was born in Bradford on 29 July 1850. She was the second child and oldest daughter in the family seven children born between 1848 and 1862, to John Fearnley Bonnell (born in Bradford in 1819), and his wife, Alice Elizabeth (formerly Duffill, born in London in 1826). They married in Bradford on 17 January 1848. The Bonnell family had been established as a harness and saddlery business in Bradford going back for 300 years.

At the time of the 1851 census the family were living at 18 Bridge Street in Bradford, and they may have resided at 17 St James's Square in Bradford, but by the time of the 1861 census they lived at 13 Edmund Street in the Horton District of Bradford. A decade later her mother and sister Jane lived at 16 Ashgrove in Bradford, but Lily was recorded as a visitor at an address at Wavertree in Liverpool.

Lily's father had died on 1 December 1876, and her mother died on 27 February 1896, so Lily and her unmarried sisters settled at 17 Welbeck Road in Birkdale, Southport. For the 1901 and 1911 censuses Lily was described as a spinster living on her own means. In fact she and her sisters were members of the committee of the Mary Willetts Excursionists' Day Nursery, which had been opened on the sands close to the pier by the then Mayoress of Southport, Mary Willetts, in 1908. It was to provide a safe place for the children of day-trippers and other visitors to the town to be looked after.

Lily was also a prominent member of the South and East Branch of the Womens' Unionist League, which had been established in 1903; and a member of the General Council. She was well-known in musical circles, having been a member of the chorus that a few weeks before she joined *Titanic* gave a performance of Elgar's *Kingdom*, at the Chapel Street Congregational Church, and she was also a member of St James's Church in Birkdale.

Caroline Bonnell was the daughter of her deceased oldest brother, John Meek, who had become a successful iron and steel merchant in Chicago, and his wife, Emily (formerly Wick). Lily's two other brothers, Harry and Joe, had also made their lives in the States.

Caroline was visiting Europe on a pleasure trip with some of her father's in-laws. They were Colonel George Wick and his wife, Mary 'Mollie', and their daughter, Mary Natalie. They had agreed to meet Lily at Southampton on 10 April to board *Titanic* as first-class passengers to accompany her back to Ohio for what she planned to be a six-month visit to see her brothers. Lily occupied cabin C103.

The Bonnells stayed at the Waldorf-Astoria Hotel in New York after the disaster, and Lily filed a claim for $1,500 against the White Star Line for loss of property.

She lived with her two sisters, Jennie and Mary, in Welbeck Road for the remainder of her life, although she continued to travel. On 24 May 1930 she left Southampton aboard the *Laconia* bound for New York; and on 1 August of the same year she is recorded as arriving in Liverpool from Bombay aboard the *Franconia*.

Jane Ellen died in 1915; Lily died on 20 February 1936, aged eighty-four, and Mary died in 1942, and all three are buried together in Birkdale Cemetery.

Dai Bowen and Leslie Williams

David John Bowen, known as Dai, had been born at Treherbert in Glamorgan, South Wales, on 30 July 1891. He was the second of three sons to James Bowen (born in about 1841), and his wife Leah (formerly Protheroe, born in 1855). They had married in 1873, and had eight children between 1876 and 1894. The 1891 census records the family as living at 35 Bagnall Street in Treherbert. A decade later they had moved to the house next door and James Bowen had died. Dai's Uncle John (Protheroe) was the publican at the nearby Royal Oak Hotel, and Leah remarried in 1902, to become Mrs Morris Owen.

At the time of the 1911 census the family lived at 42 Bagnall Street, and Dai was described as an unmarried coal miner, it might be worth explaining this term, I had to google it.

Dai decided to take up boxing, and came under the guidance of George Cundick, who had learned the art of pugilism as a physical trainer with the British Army in India. Dai had fought eight bouts between April 1910 and November 1911, winning three, two by knockout, losing two on points, and drawing one. Most of his fights were at the Millfield Athletic Club in Pontypridd, although his last two were in the North-East.

Dai and Leslie Williams booked their passage through the Dean and Dawson Tourist and Steamship Company in Cardiff, and they paid extra for the third-class tickets so that they could have use of the first-class gymnasium to keep themselves in shape during the voyage. They should have boarded the *Lusitania*, but Leslie had ordered new suits and wanted to wait until they arrived, so they were given passage on the brand new luxury liner *Titanic* for its maiden voyage.

Leslie Williams was born at Tonypandy in Glamorgan, South Wales, during the summer of 1888. He was the fourth and youngest son of Albert Clive Williams and his wife, Mary Jane (formerly Thomas), who had married in about 1873. They had eight surviving children born between 1875 and 1891.

Leslie first appears on the 1891 census, when the family was living at 4 Fearnley Terrace in Clydach, Ystradyfodwg, in the Rhondda Valley, and a decade later they had moved to 19 Gleaner Street. Although Leslie was only twelve years old, he had left school and was working as an apprentice boilermaker.

In 1910 he married Lillie Thomas (born at Tonypandy on 1 July 1891), and a son named Leslie James was born to them on 29 October 1910. In 1911 they lived at 59 Primrose Street in Tonypandy. When Leslie left for Southampton, Lillie was pregnant with their second child.

Les began working as a blacksmith, but he decided to take up boxing as a profession, and his ring weight was 8st 10lb, or bantamweight. He had fought in twelve bouts between March 1908 and December 1911, winning six, all on points, and losing two, being knocked out in his last fight. He had also drawn one, had a no contest decision, and was disqualified in another. He too had fought several bouts at the Millfield Athletic Club, and he had also fought twice in Paris.

Dai Bowen's body was never recovered, but Leslie was body number 14 picked up by the *Mackay-Bennett* on 22 April 1912. He was identified by his effects. He was wearing a green overcoat over a blue serge suit, with a red striped shirt and two scarves. He had on his person two gold rings, a pair of silver cufflinks, a knife, two pocket books, papers, a ticket, and an amount of money in dollar gold, pounds and pennies. His possessions were returned to his wife, who wanted his remains to be brought back to Wales for burial, but unfortunately his body was buried at sea. Two pennies from the year 1899 and 1900 were retrieved by the family as treasured mementoes. A benefit to help the families was held at the Mid-Rhondda Athletic Grounds on 22 April 1912, consisting of a gymkhana and assault-at-arms tournament, and numerous well-known boxers supported the cause.

Lillie gave birth to a son named Harold Charles on 25 July 1912. According to family history, a local coal miner named Dan Winter had promised that if anything should happen to Leslie he would look after Lillie. He kept to his word and they married in 1914, having several more children.

Dai's family paid for a grave site memorial dedicated to him which was erected in Treorchy Cemetery, and his brother Stephen wrote the epitaph:

> In loving memory of my dear brother David John Bowen.
> No more I'll see him in our midst, no more his voice I'll hear,
> For death has been and taken away the one I loved so dear.
> Twilight and evening bell, and after that the dark,
> And may there be no sadness or farewell when it embark.
> Some day, some time my eyes shall see thy loving face.
> Never shall your memory fade.

Of the sportsmen who survived the tragedy, tennis player Dick Williams went on to win the United States Mixed Doubles Championship later in the year. He also won the singles in 1914 and 1916, and the doubles in 1925 and 1926. He won the 1920 Wimbledon doubles title in 1920. At the 1924 Paris Olympic Games he won the mixed doubles gold medal despite having to play on with a sprained ankle. He captained several United States Davis Cup teams, and he was inducted into the International Tennis Hall of Fame in 1957. He died in 1968, the first year of Open tennis.

John Ryerson became a successful amateur golfer. He played in 400 tournaments and on a record 1,000 golf courses. He died in 1986.

William Theodore Ronald Brailey

William Brailey, known as Theo, was born at Walthamstow in Essex, on 25 October 1887, the oldest child of four, to William Richard Brailey (born in Plymouth in 1863), and his wife, Amy Jane (formerly Greenwood – born in London on 28 December 1869, died in Kensington on 11 November 1941). They had married at West Ham in 1887, and among his father's various professions were an insurance superintendent and a clairvoyant. He had been a Baptist minister turned spiritualist.

At the time of his birth the family home was at 18 Clarendon Road in Walthamstow. Theo had three younger sisters named Mabel Violet (born in 1890, died in 1982); Lily Sunshine (born in 1893); and Daphne Olive Vera Eileen (born in 1909, died in 1986). In the 1891 census the family were recorded as living at 69 William Street in Upton, Slough, and a decade later they had moved to 36 Merton Road at Leyton in Essex. By 1911 they had moved into London, the family home being at 71 Lancaster Road in Ladbroke Grove, Kensington, west London, and Theo was described as an unmarried pianist and professor of music.

Theo and his sisters were encouraged to play the piano and took music lessons from a woman named Miriam Geary. Theo displayed musical talent, not only on the piano, but also with the cello and flute. He eventually joined the Kensington Palace Hotel Orchestra.

With his father's consent he decided to join the army and he enlisted into the Lancashire Fusiliers on 9 October 1902, serving in Barbados with the unit during the riots and assassinations caused by economic collapse that took place there. He was appointed bandsman, and he discharged on 22 February 1907 after four years' service.

After military service he decided to take his music more seriously, and he is known to have composed at least two pieces of music – *Ballet of the Roses* and *A Little Scherzo*. Although his family were in London, Theo stayed in Southport, having become interested in aviation, which at that time was in its infancy. He also met and became engaged to Teresa 'Terry' Steinhilber (born in Southport in 1889), who was the daughter of a German-born Southport watchmaker named August Steinhilber and his wife Kate.

The *Liverpool Echo* of 25 April 1912, stated:

> Our photo is of Mr William T Brailey, who was a member of the now famous and heroic orchestra of *Titanic*. Mr Brailey was at one time associated with Mr Compton Paterson (a well-known aviation pioneer, who in 1910 became the first man to fly a passenger plane across the River Mersey) at the Freshfield Aerodrome (in Formby), and Mr John Gaunt at the Southport hangar. He was also a member of the Southport Pier Pavilion Band (for two years). He was engaged to a well-known Southport young lady named Miss Steinhilber of St Luke's Road in Southport.

He took up employment as a musician aboard RMS *Saxonia*, and ironically, he and Roger Bricoux served on the Cunard steamer *Carpathia* before joining the White Star Line.

If Theo's body was recovered it was never identified.

Harold Sidney Bride

Harold Bride was interviewed for the *New York Times* less than a week after the disaster in the presence of Guglielmo Marconi, and stated 'I was born in Nunhead, London SE, twenty-two years ago, and joined the Marconi staff last July. I first worked on the *Haverford*, and then on the *Lusitania*, and was transferred to the RMS *Titanic* at Belfast.' Nunhead now forms part of Peckham in the London borough of Southwark.

Harold was born on 11 January 1890, the youngest of four sons in the family of seven children to a merchant named Arthur John Larner Bride (1852-1921) and his wife, Mary Ann (formerly Lowe, 1847-1927). His siblings were all born between 1874 and 1887. He was known to be quite shy and soft spoken.

In 1903 the family moved to live at 58 Ravensbourne Avenue near Shortlands Golf Course in Bromley. It was here in 1910 that he first began putting his interest of wireless telegraphy into practice. He erected an antenna and strung sires from the house to the garden shed, from where he practiced Morse Code. He trained as a Marconi operator at the British School of Telegraphy on Clapham Road, and on gaining a Government certificate in July 1911 he went to sea.

Harold's first job was on the SS *Haverford*, an American transatlantic ship bound for Philadelphia, then on the SS *Beaverford*, a cargo liner operated by the Canadian Pacific Steamship Company. He went to Brazil three times on the *Le France*, a transatlantic liner with the French Line; twice to New York on the ocean liner RMS *Lusitania*; and two more times to Brazil on the SS *Anseim*, a cargo and passenger liner sailing between Liverpool and South America.

On 16 March 1912, he became engaged to a nurse named Mabel Ludlow, but he broke off the engagement on his return from Australia on 25 September 1912.

He and Jack Phillips, who hailed from Godalming in Surrey, joined *Titanic* at Belfast and sailed with her to Southampton, where Harold stayed at the *Bannisters Hotel*, and he signed on the ship on 9 April, for wages of £4 a month.

He was rescued in collapsible B dinghy, which was in the charge of Charles Lightoller, and included Algernon Barkworth and Charles Joughin.

On arriving in New York on *Carpathia* Harold spent some time in hospital suffering from badly frozen and crushed feet. It was also reported that he spent some time recovering at the home of a family named Jarvis. It seems that some of his family had moved to New York and changed their name to Jarvis.

His father was obviously a thoughtful man of high principles and he sent a letter to the *New York Times* thanking all those involved in saving his son's life and for looking after his welfare afterwards.

The London via Melbourne records of August 1912, state that he was a wireless operator on the SS *Medina*. On arriving in Sydney on 8 August, he is reported to have given a 'Graphic Story of the Wreck' to various newspapers. However, a week later, under the heading 'A Silent Hero', when asked to tell his story again he refused, saying to one reporter on board the *Medina* 'If you wait here all night I will not say a word.'

One of the paragraphs in his story in the Australian newspapers was perhaps a bit more graphic than it should have been, and it may be that the reporters wished to pursue this incident more than Harold felt comfortable with:

> Something happened now that I hate to tell about. I was back in my room getting Phillips's money for him. As I looked out of the door I saw a stoker or somebody, from below decks leaning over Phillips' from behind. Phillips was too busy to notice what the man

> was doing. He was slipping the lifebelt off Phillips's back. He was a big man, too, and as you can see I am very small. I don't know what it was I got hold of. I remembered in a flash the way Phillips had clung on. How I had to fix that lifebelt in place because he was too busy to do it. I know that the man from below decks had his own lifebelt and should have known where to get it. I suddenly felt a passion not to let that man die a decent sailor's death. I wished he might have stretched a rope or walked the plank. I did my duty. I hope I finished him; I don't know. We left him on the cabin floor of the wireless room, and he wasn't moving.

During the Great War Harold served as a wireless operator on the SS *Mona's Isle*, and it is also said that he worked on cross-Channel ferries out of Dover.

He met a twenty-three-year-old Scottish girl named Lucy Johnstone Downie. Lucy worked as a teacher in London, so Harold took a job in the city so that they could be together.

Harold continued to dislike discussing the events concerning the disaster and he had been deeply disturbed by the incident, particularly because of the loss of his friend Jack Phillips, who he considered to be one of the heroes of the disaster. He eventually decided to get away from the attention that being a *Titanic* survivor attracted, and he and Lucy moved to the Stranraer area of Wigtownshire, on the south-west coast of Scotland, her father's native town.

They married on 10 April 1920, and Harold became a travelling salesman for a pharmaceuticals company based at Hanover Street in Stranraer. They lived in the village of Garlieston, and Lucy was born in 1921, John was born in 1924, and Janette was born in 1929. His unwanted celebrity status seems to have followed him even there and they moved a few times. They went to live in Mansfield Road at Scone near Perth, in 1934, and then 16 miles to Dunning ten years later, where they remained for four years. They later moved to Proven Hall in Stepps, north-east of Glasgow, where Harold is said to have operated his own radio as a hobby.

Harold died of lung cancer on 29 April 1956, aged sixty-six, in Stobhill General Hospital in the Canmore district of Glasgow. He was cremated at the Glasgow Crematorium and his ashes were scattered in the chapel garden of remembrance. His wife died on 9 August 1973, at Prestwick in Ayrshire, and Janette died on 3 January 1991, at Ashford in Kent.

Arthur Bride had died in 1921 and they had to sell the house in Bromley in the following year. A commemoration blue plaque was placed at the house in 2004. Harold was depicted by a twenty-seven-year-old Lancastrian named Craig Kelly in James Cameron's 1997 film *Titanic*.

John Butterworth

John Butterworth (known as Jack) gave his place of birth as Manchester when he signed on as a saloon steward to *Titanic* and stated his age as twenty-three. He had red hair, and was the son of William James Butterworth and his wife, Mary. It would seem that he was a keen football fan.

Jack had previously served on the SS *New York*. He lived in Southampton, where he had been courting May Hinton, who was from Woolston in Southampton, and they had agreed to become engaged. His last given address was 270 Priory Road in St Denys, Southampton, which was the home of the Kellaway family.

May received a letter from Jack on 20 April 1912, her twenty-first birthday – she also received notification from the White Star Line that day that he was not among the survivors. Jack's body was number 116 recovered by the *Mackay-Bennett*. He was described as having red hair, and he was wearing dark clothes with a white steward's jacket and black boots. He had a cigarette case on his person. His remains were buried at sea on 24 April. His father was listed as a Class D dependent in the Mansion House Relief Fund documents.

Clear Annie Cameron

Clear Cameron was born on 8 March 1877, at 20 Higham View in Pendleton, Salford, the daughter of Harry Arthur Cameron (born in Leek in 1846, died in Buxton on 2 May 1899), and his wife, Annie (formerly Childs, born at Kemberton in Shropshire in 1846, died soon after her husband in Buxton on 22 June 1899). Harry was a master tailor, and they had married at the Mill Street Chapel in Leamington Spa, Warwickshire, on 24 May 1872. Clear had an older brother named Ernest (1870-1945) and a sister named Janet Gertrude (born in Leamington on 18 February 1873, died in Bournemouth as Mrs Dowding on 28 March 1914).

By 1881 they had moved to live at 73 London Road in Buxton, where her sister, Nic, was born in 1883. By 1891 their home was at the same address, but fourteen-year-old Clear was working as a housemaid at 117 London Road.

Her desire for higher wages eventually took her to London, where she gained employment as personal maid at Hyde Park Gate in Kensington, the home of Colonel Henry Hugh Oldham CVO, and his wife, Ella.

Clear befriended Ellen 'Nellie' Walcroft. In order to earn more money, Nellie had decided to go to her sisters, who lived on a farm at Mamaroneck in New York, and she asked Clear to go with her. Apparently there should have been a third girl on the trip with them but she had to cancel. They had booked their passage on another liner, but the ship was held up because of the coal strike and they were transferred to *Titanic*. Nellie recalled how they had stayed in London and caught the special train to Southampton. They shared a second-class cabin on E-deck. Clear corresponded with her sister Janet, and in a letter dated 21 April 1912, she told her story of the disaster.

They were met by Nellie's sister and brother-in-law, Carl Land, who was a chauffeur and had been lent his employer's family car to collect the girls. On arriving at the farm, Nellie sent a cablegram to her parents in Maidenhead, expressing something of an understatement: 'Arrived, well, Nellie.' When the *Carpathia* docked in New York, Clear stated her age to be thirty-one, but she was actually four years older, and she seems to have been in the habit of knocking a few years off in matters concerning her age.

Clear never received any compensation for the loss of her property, which was worth over £1,000. She was at Haverford in Pennsylvania in October 1913, and she remained in the States for some time. She married a butler named Ernest William Francis in Philadelphia on 29 April 1914.

Clear returned to England, and suffering with senility, she spent her last years at the Knaphill Nursing Home in Woking, Surrey, where she died of cardiovascular degeneration and senility (heart failure) on 2 February 1962. The death certificate gives her age as seventy-eight, but she was actually just a month short of her eighty-fifth birthday. Her funeral took place at the Woking St John Crematorium, and her ashes were scattered on the Keats Garden. Ernest died soon afterwards, on 17 September 1962.

In 1999 Clear's collection of letters sold for £60,000, and in 2002 a small photograph taken of her before she left for America sold for £7,700.

John Frederick Preston Clarke

'Fred' Clarke was born at 2 Churchill Terrace in Chorlton-cum-Hardy, Manchester, on 28 July 1883. He was the only son and oldest of three children of a law stationer (clerk) named John Robert Clarke (born at Croydon in Surrey in 1865), and his wife, Ellen (formerly Preston, born at Sandal in Wakefield, Yorkshire in 1861), who was a dressmaker. His sisters were Ellen Mary (born in 1885) and Emily Florence (born in 1887).

He had a maternal aunt named Elizabeth, who was described as a musician on the 1891 census. She married the violinist Vasco Ackeroyd and Fred became his pupil. His father and Uncle Edward fled to America, and the 1901 census states that he lived at 174 Tunstall Street, off Smithdown Road in Liverpool, and by 1911 he had moved to 22 Tunstall Road.

He embarked on *Titanic* at Southampton on 10 April 1912 to take up an appointment as bass violist with the ship's orchestra. John died in the disaster, and his body was number 202 recovered by the *Mackay-Bennett*, and buried at Mount Olivet Cemetery in Halifax on 8 May 1912. He was wearing a grey overcoat, a grey muffler, a uniform with green facings and green socks. The body had a crucifix around the neck. His effects consisted of a diamond pin, a gold watch, a gold ring marked 'JFPC', a set of keys, a sovereign case, a knife, a pocket book, a memo book, and eight shillings.

The *Birkenhead News* for 20 April 1912, reported:

> One of those on board *Titanic* and who it is feared is amongst those who have perished, is Mr JFP Clarke, formerly a member of the orchestra of the Argyle Theatre of Varieties (in Birkenhead). Mr Clarke in his short time played the bass at the theatre. He then got employment with the White Star Line and was appointed as a member of the orchestra formed to render music on the ill-fated *Titanic*. He was in Birkenhead in the early part of last week, and said good-bye to friends preparatory to leaving for Southampton to join *Titanic*. Mr. Clarke is very well known in musical circles. Only two Saturdays ago he was in Birkenhead and was very well. He attended the performance at the Argyle Theatre and met a number of friends there.
>
> He appeared rather morose and he said had hopes of receiving great benefit from his voyage on *Titanic*. After completing his services with the White Star Company, he hoped to embark on a musical season again. He was an enthusiastic musician, and has played in the Liverpool Philharmonic band. He had a large circle of friends in Birkenhead. The survivors from Titanic are loud in their praise of the members of the orchestra. After the collision

> they brought their instruments on deck and played almost until the moment that the ship broke in two and foundered. The last item of a concert such as surely has never taken place in the history of the sea is reported to have been 'Nearer My God to Thee'.

The Journal of Lever Brothers at Port Sunlight for July 1912 reported:

> Mr Fred Clarke of *Titanic*'s band, whose performances up to the last moment will live in the history of the disaster, was for many years a familiar and popular ally of our Philharmonic Society at their special concerts. Villagers will easily recall his appearance at the Coronation Concert. Many who knew him had a melancholy satisfaction in attending a special benefit performance in aid of his mother and sisters which was held at the Philharmonic Hall in Liverpool, in May.

Mary Elizabeth Davison

Mary Elizabeth Finkenagel was born at Malmesbury in Wiltshire, on 19 February 1878. She was the third daughter and seventh child of ten born between 1862 and 1886 to Thomas Finkenagel (born in Germany in 1837), and his wife, Elizabeth (born at Rochdale in 1841). They had married at Stroud in Gloucestershire, on 2 October 1858. Thomas eventually shortened the family name to Finck.

The family lived for a short while at Westport St Mary near Malmesbury, before moving to the bigger town in about 1873 to take over the running of a boarding house on Church Street. Mary's parents and much of the family went to live in Cleveland in Ohio, United States, where her brother, John, lived at 2256 East 69th Street.

In 1902 she married a blacksmith named Thomas Henry Davison. 'Harry' had been born at Chippenham in Wiltshire on 27 February 1880, the second son of eight in the family of eleven children born between 1876 and 1896, of a corn miller named Thomas Cook Henry Davison (born in Swindon on 8 January 1859, died in 1931), and his wife, Sarah Ann (formerly Long, born at Langley Burrell near Chippenham in 1856, died in 1935). The Davison family lived on Sheldon Road in Chippenham, then at 32 Marshfield Road, and by 1901 they had moved to a house called 'Woodlands' in Hardenhuish on the outskirts of Chippenham.

Mary and Harry lived at 32 Marshfield Road in Chippenham, and they had two children who both died in infancy. One of them was named after his father and died in 1907. They travelled to visit Mary's family in Cleveland in 1908, and they decided to move to Bedford near Cleveland. They are known to have travelled to Liverpool, probably to board a different ship, because they gave their last known address as Liverpool, but they boarded *Titanic* in Southampton as third-class passengers.

It is believed that Mary was rescued in boat 16, but Harry died in the sinking, and if his body was recovered it was never identified.

Mary is not recorded as ever returning to England. On 29 July 1913, at Warrensville Heights, she married Ohio-born Fred Buesher (1881-1944), but they were soon divorced, and on 6 September 1917, she married Henry Godwin (born in 1879); who had moved from her home town in 1910. They lived at 12821 Martson Street in Cleveland.

Mary died of cancer on 26 March 1939, aged sixty-one, and she lies buried in Bedford Cemetery. Henry died on 7 November 1950, and is buried with her. The skirt she wore when she was evacuated from the stricken ship is still in the possession of the family.

Albert George Ervine

Albert Ervine, known as Bertie, was born at Clement Vale in Rosetta Park, south Belfast, on 2 August 1893. He was the second son of four in the family of six children born between 1887 and 1905 to a poor rate collector named Albert Ervine (born in County Down on 1 March 1860) and his wife Helene Jane (formerly Gowans, born in Perth on 19 January 1862). Albert and Helen married in Perth in 1887.

They eventually moved to Ireland, where they lived at Ballynahinch in County Down, before settling in Belfast in the late 1880s. At the time of the 1901 census they lived at 1 Old Cavehill Road in the Clifton area of north Belfast. The family were known as Brethrens, non-conformist Evangelical Christians. Bertie was educated at the nearby Belfast Royal Academy, and then at the Methodist (Methody) College in south Belfast, and then at the Municipal Technical Institute. He spent part of his apprenticeship with Coombe, Barber and Coombe, before going to the Harland and Wolff shipyard to study marine electronics.

At the time of the 1911 census the family had moved along the road to a house called 'Merryfield' at number 16, where Bertie was described as an unmarried electrician. Ireland was on the verge of the Home Rule crisis, especially in Belfast, and was becoming increasingly tense because of sectarian issues. Albert was stated to be a Protestant, possibly to identify himself as a Unionist.

He worked on the construction of SS *Maloja*, which was completed on 7 September 1911, and he sailed with her on her maiden voyage as a passenger liner with P and O.

He and his friend, Alfred Middleton, another member of the Brethren, then petitioned the White Star Line to be transferred to *Titanic* for her maiden voyage. They were on the vessel for its delivery to Southampton and when he officially signed on he was the youngest member of the engineering department.

Albert lost his life in the disaster and if his body was recovered it was never identified. On the first anniversary of his death, the Belfast newsletter had the following memorial:

> Ervine: In loving memory of Bertie, the loving and beloved son of Albert and Helene Jane Ervine, who perished with the SS *Titanic* in mid-Atlantic on 15 April 1912. 'Oh, the depth of the niches, both of the wisdom and knowledge of God! How unsearchable are His judgements, and His ways past finding out! – Rom, XI, 33.'

Most of Albert's siblings moved to North America, and his mother died in Florida in 1942. His father was the recipient of his estate, and he also received money from the Mansion House fund. He died in Blackpool in 1953.

Henry Samuel Etches

Harry Etches was born in the Freemantle district of Southampton, on 12 October 1868. He was the second son and fourth child of eleven of a Scotsman named John George Etches (born in 1829, died in 1887), and his wife, Caroline Elizabeth (formerly Newman, born at Southampton in 1833, died in 1902). They had married in Southampton in 1853. Their children were born between 1854 and 1875.

The family first appear on the 1871 census as living at 68 Park Road in Millbrook, Southampton, and his father was described as a master painter. A decade later Harry was not recorded as living with the family, and his widowed mother was living as a boarder at 47 St Mary's Road in Southampton.

At Bermondsey in London, on New Year's Day of 1896, Harry married a farmer's daughter named Lilian Rachel Smith (born at Thockmorton, Pershore near Worcester in 1873). Harry was absent from the 1901 census, but his wife was recorded as a visitor at 114 Derby Road in St Mary's, Southampton, and a decade later she was living at 23A Gordon Avenue in the district of Portswood, Southampton.

Harry had served on *Olympic*, and he had been serving on RMS *Oruba* when he signed on *Titanic* as a bedroom steward, his station being at the aft portside of B Deck, where he was in charge of eight cabins, and the cabin of Thomas Andrews on A Deck.

The *Evesham Journal* of 20 April 1912 reported that Harry was one of the missing. On arriving in New York he was called to give evidence at the American Senate enquiry. He journeyed back to England on the *Adriatic*, and arrived in Liverpool on 11 May.

He is said to have taken two more trips aboard *Olympic*, and during the Great War he was assigned to *Britannic*, after it had been converted into a hospital ship. It is believed that he survived a second shipping disaster when *Britannic* was torpedoed in 1916.

He eventually left the service, and he and his wife settled in her home town of Pershore, where they lived at Eaton Villa in the district of Fladbury. He died there of heart failure/disease (chronic myocarditis) on 30 September 1944, aged seventy-five. His wife died in 1954. The Pershore Heritage Centre has what they believe to be the black woollen hat Harry wore during his ordeal aboard *Titanic*.

Frederick Fleet

Frederick Fleet was born in Liverpool on 15 October 1887. He never knew his father, and his mother, Alice, who lived at 19 Birchfield Road in Walton, is believed to have abandoned him and went to live in the United States.

Consequently, Fred was raised by a succession of foster families and distant relatives via orphanages and Dr Barnardo Homes. At the age of twelve he was sent to a training ship, where he stayed until he was sixteen. He went to sea as a deck boy, working his way up to able seaman. Before signing on *Titanic* he had sailed for over four years as lookout on *Oceanic*. His address was given as Norman Road in Southampton. Fred earned an extra five shillings on top of his salary for lookout duty, and it was as a lookout that he joined *Titanic* in April 1912. Fred appeared as a witness before both the United States Senate and the British Board of Trade Inquiries.

From June 1912, Fred served briefly as seaman on the White Star liner *Olympic*. He found that White Star looked at the surviving officers and crew as embarrassing reminders of the recent disaster and he left the company in August 1912. For the next twenty-four years he sailed with Union-Castle and various other companies, retiring from the sea in 1936. He then worked for Harland and Wolff as a shipbuilder, and later was the shore Master-at-Arms for the Union-Castle Mail Steamship Company.

He married Annie Clark, and had a son name Alfred. In later life he sold newspapers on the corner of Pound Tree Road in Southampton, and lived with his wife's brother. Fred's wife died on 28 December 1964 and her brother evicted him. In a state of despondency, he hanged himself in Norman Road, Freemantle, Southampton, his body being discovered on 10 January 1965. He was aged seventy-six, and was buried in an unmarked grave at Hollybrook Cemetery in Southampton.

In 1993, a headstone was erected by Titanic Historical Society. In the 1997 film *Titanic* he was portrayed by Scott G Anderson, a twenty-five-year-old Englishman.

Joseph John Fynney

Joseph Fynney was born at Great Sutton near Ellesmere Port in Cheshire during the second half of 1876. He was the youngest child of a cow keeper and dairyman named Richard Fynney (born at Wetton in Staffordshire in 1828), and his wife, Frances (formerly Windsor, born at Maryport in Cumberland on 8 September 1840). They were married in Liverpool in 1872. Joe's siblings were John (born in 1873); and Martha Jane (born in 1874, later Mrs Bruce Hoseason).

They eventually moved to Liverpool and had lived at 68 Upper Parliament Street in Toxteth, and at 4 Crump Street in Toxteth, and they lived at 168 Brownlow Hill in Liverpool when Richard died on 16 July 1894. They had moved to 6 Sandon Street in Waterloo by 1901, and at the time of the 1911 census his brother and sister had gone to live at Montreal in Canada, and he was living with his elderly mother at a house called Brookfield in Park Way, Liverpool. He was employed as an India rubber merchant with his own firm of Joseph J Fynney and Company, but he also worked with delinquents at the Anglican Church of St James, off Upper Parliament Street in Toxteth. Close to the church lived a young lad named (William) Alfred Gaskell, at 20 Dexter Street. Alfred had been baptised at St James's on 3 May 1893, and he had followed in his father's footsteps as a cooper (barrel maker).

It seems that Joe spent a lot of his time in the company of young boys, and neighbours are known to have complained about the comings and goings of young men to his house on Park Way.

Joe and Alfred boarded *Titanic* at Southampton on 10 April 1912, on the same ticket and they shared a cabin. They both died in the disaster. If Alfred's body was recovered it was never identified, and Joe's body was recovered from the sea by the SS *Minia* on 3 May 1912, being listed as body number 322.

A document concerning the recovery of his body held at the Nova Scotia Archives described him as having black hair, a smooth face, being a height of 5ft 6in, and having the following effects upon him: six £5 Bank of England notes, 7/6 in silver, pocket handkerchief, neckerchief, memorandum book, London and North Western railway ticket, silver knife, pencil in case, cigar holder, and letters.

He was buried at Mount Royal Cemetery in Montreal. His memorial says: 'In loving memory of Joseph Fynney of Liverpool, Eng. Aged 35 years who lost his life at R.M.S. *Titanic* Disaster April 15, 1912 and was found May 3, 1912. His delight was in doing good.'

His name is also included on the grave of his father at Anfield Cemetery in Liverpool. The memorial says: 'Lost on RMS *Titanic*, 15th April 1912, aged 35 years, and was interned at Montreal. Nearer My God to Thee.' His mother died in Toronto on 16 January 1916, and is buried by his side.

Arthur Henry Gee

Arthur Gee was born on 21 March 1865, at 25 Bolton Road, Irlams o' th' Height, Pendleton, Salford, the son of Giles Gee, who was a calico print dyer, and his wife, Amelia (formerly Crosby). He had three older siblings; Walter (born in Eccles in 1853), William (born in Eccles in 1857), and Emily (born in Salford in 1863).

He was taken to Russia by his parents when he was three, and spent his early years at Schlisselburg near St Petersburg, where his father was employed at the local calico printing works. At the age of fourteen he came back to live on the Height for the purpose of pursuing his studies at the Manchester Grammar School, and he attended the United Methodist Sunday School. He was also a member of the chapel choir.

His father sent him to Alsace in Germany to study the chemistry of calico printing, and while he was there he learned to speak French and German.

After finishing his studies, he returned to Schlisselburg, where he was employed at the calico printing works, working his way up to become the manager.

On returned to England in about 1911 he settled at Morningside, Riley Avenue, St Anne's-on-Sea, Lancashire, with his wife, Edith, and his fifteen-year-old daughter and three younger sons. He took employment as a representative for the firm of Whitehead, Sumner, Harker and Company, machinery exporters based in Deansgate in Manchester. He enjoyed playing golf on the St Anne's Old Links Golf Course on Highbury Road.

Arthur had apparently organised the trip across the Atlantic to take a job as manager of a linen mill near Mexico City, after which he was contemplating retiring. He intended to sail from Liverpool, but because industrial unrest had affected the port there the ship was delayed and, as fate would have it, he happily agreed to travel to Southampton to board the brand-new luxury liner RMS *Titanic*.

During the voyage, Arthur kept a diary in the form of an eight-page letter, which records the daily mileage of the ship, details about the food and the people he met. He records that on 13 April he was moved to another cabin by a steward because he wanted a porthole. The cabin was arranged for four people, with two wardrobes, large sofa, chest of drawers, three electric lights, electric fan and heater. The porthole was 15ft from the water line.

He had dined with Purser McElroy, and on the night of the disaster he sat with two businessmen, an American named Charles Jones, and Algernon Barkworth, in the first-class smoking room. They had a conversation about road building, before he went to bed. Barkworth stated:

> Coming over I made the acquaintance of two most agreeable chaps … The other man was A H Gee. I was discussing in the smoking room with them late on Sunday night the science of good road building in which I am keenly interested. When the crash came somebody said we had hit an iceberg, but I didn't see it.

Arthur was reported to be a strong swimmer but he drowned in the sinking. His body was number 275 recovered from the water by the *Mackay-Bennett*, being described as aged about sixty, although he was actually forty-seven, having dark hair and a moustache. He was wearing a brown overcoat, with a tuxedo suit and dress pants. His effects were a silver watch, gold chain, silver cigarette case, various small items and some banknotes.

His eldest brother, Walter, who had stayed on in Moscow as manager of the calico works, died at about the same time as *Titanic* was lost. Arthur's remains arrived in New York and were transported to Liverpool on the *Baltic*. His funeral took place on 18 May at St John's Church, on the Height in Salford, and he was buried in the grave next to his father. The gravestone stood for some time but has now been removed and the area has been grassed over.

'Kate Gold'

Kate Gold was born as Jane Kate Coulson at 80 King Street in Woolwich, on 19 April 1866, and she was baptised on 3 June that year at St Mary Magdalene's Church in Greenwich. She was the daughter of Staff Sergeant Charles Coulson of the Royal Artillery and Priscilla Booker (formerly Wright, born at Bath in Somerset in 1831, died in 1911), who had married on 14 June 1865. Her mother was previously married in 1857, to Sergeant William Booker, who had also served with the Royal Artillery, and they had a daughter named Elizabeth, born in 1860, who was at boarding school in Kenilworth, Warwickshire, in 1871.

By 1881 the family home was at Cambridge Cottages in Woolwich (known as the Royal Engineers Huts), and Kate is recorded as a visitor at the home of her cousin, Benjamin Cork and his wife, at Canal Side in Burton upon Trent, Staffordshire. She was an apprentice dressmaker, known as Kate, the name she used on *Titanic*.

Her father had died by 1881, and her mother had to move out of the military accommodation in Woolwich. She became the first district nurse for Southport, and she was recorded as working as a night nurse at the Southport Infirmary and Dispensary in Virginia Street, North Moels. A decade later, Kate was living with her mother at 117 Shakespeare Street in North Moels., and she is still described as a dressmaker.

On 12 November 1892 she married John Hannah Gold (born in Salford in 1868, died in Liverpool in 1949), at St Paul's Church in Southport. John lived at 34 Prince's Street in Southport, and he was described as a commercial traveller.

They moved to Liverpool, where they lived at 40 Crosby Green in West Derby. They both began careers serving at sea, but by the time of the 1911 census they were separated, and Kate is recorded as a visitor at 31 Underhill

Street in Everton, and described herself as a widowed stewardess on the Southampton to New York run.

Kate worked for the White Star Line, serving on several ships, including the *Teutonic*, *Suevic*, *Adriatic* and *Olympic*. *The St Anne's Express* newspaper of Lancashire, for 19 April 1912, stated:

> A Southport lady who was on the ill-fated *Titanic*, Mrs K Gold, stewardess, had been in three accidents. She was on board the *Suevic* when that vessel was wrecked returning from Australia, (It ran aground off the Lizard Peninsula in 1907). Her second experience was on the *Olympic* two or three months ago, when that vessel was in collision with HMS *Hawke*.

When she signed on *Titanic* as a first-class stewardess she gave her address as Glenthorne Bassett in Southampton. Kate was assigned to cabins on B deck, and was once again working with her friend, Annie Martin. Among the passengers they would wait on were a family whose two dogs came to the stewardess cabin every morning to see them.

The Western Daily Mercury newspaper of Plymouth, for 30 April 1912, reported:

> shortly before the special train streamed out of the docks, two of the stewardesses who are returning to their homes, Mrs Gold and Ms Martin granted a brief interview, in which they narrated their experiences. They were first class stewardesses on *Titanic*, and were both saved in number 11 boat. They had been old shipmates, having sailed together in the *Olympic* and *Adriatic*, whilst in their earlier careers they were both in the *Cedric*, of the same line.

After arriving in New York, Kate and Annie returned to England on the *Lapland*. She was detained by the British authorities, in order to take her statement. She signed off the ship's articles on 30 April 1912, her wages having ceased from the moment *Titanic* sank.

The St Anne's Express newspaper in Lancashire stated:

> And now she has been rescued from the most appalling wreck in the history of the mercantile marine. In spite of this experience,

> it is not expected that Mrs Gold will give up the life which she always declares she loves. She is a strongly-nerved woman, and the two previous accidents did not deter her in the past from continuing in the service.

In 1913 she travelled to Australia on the *Belgic* to take up an appointment as housekeeper to her uncle, Harry Wright, at Ballarat in Victoria, Australia, and while staying at the *Warren View Hotel* in Enmore, Sydney, during September 1913, she gave an interview with local newspapers, including the *Bathurst Times* for 6 September 1913. Described as 'The Heroine on the Wreck' and 'The last woman to leave the vessel', she stated 'It was fine and clear, that awful night'.

She married Ernest Patterson in 1917, at Marrickville at the inner west area of Sydney.

Several Australian newspapers for 24 January 1949 carried the following report, under the heading 'Titanic Tragedy Recalled by Heroine of Iceberg Disaster':

> The sea tragedy of 1912 involving the loss of the White Star 45,000 ton liner *Titanic* … has been recalled by the death in Dulwich Hill (Sydney) recently of Mrs Kate Patterson, aged 82.
>
> Mrs Patterson (at that time was Mrs Gold) was cared for in her declining years by Mrs N Germaine, a sister of Mr D Hooper of Wood Street, Warwick. Mrs Germaine's home in Dulwich Hill adjoins the flat in which Mrs Patterson had lived alone for a number of years.
>
> Mr Hooper himself met Mrs Patterson on different visits to Sydney, and he described her yesterday as a woman of striking personality.

Emily Esther Louise Hart

Esther Bloomfield was born on 13 May 1863, at Stockwell in Surrey (now within the borough of Lambeth in Greater London), and was christened on 16 July that year, at St Barnabas C of E church in nearby Kennington, Surrey. Her parents were a gardener named George (born in about 1844 at St Leonards in Gloucestershire), and his wife Esther (formerly Hayes, born at Cranley in Surrey). They had married at Slinfold in Sussex on 15 July 1862.

At the time of the 1871 census the family lived at Stockwell Grove in Lambeth, London, and Esther had a little sister named Alice Charlotte, and an infant brother named William Henry. Minnie, Elizabeth Mary and Henry were born later, and a sister named Kate Jane was born in 1865, but she died a year later. The 1881 census names Esther Bloomfield as a housemaid with the family of George Simpson at Herne Hill in Lambeth.

On 28 November 1881 Emily married a clerk named George Brook, and had several children, but George died in 1890.

Emily married Benjamin Hart in the West Ham district of Essex in the autumn of 1900. A daughter named Eva Miriam was born at Ilford on 31 January 1905. Eva was educated at St Mary's Convent, which later became St Mary's Hare Park at Gidea Park near Romford. In 1912 the family lived at Slinfold House, Whalebone Grove in Chadwell Heath.

Soon after the disaster a local newspaper reported:

> Ilford has her part to play in the latest tragedy of the ocean. On April 2nd last, Mr and Mrs Ben Hart were present at the 'Cauliflower' in their honour prior to their departure for Canada. During the evening they were the recipients of a beautiful Illuminated Address which included the following words: 'And may the Almighty Jahovah send you safe voyage and a prosperous career in the land of your adoption.' Mr Hart was a jew, and the introduction of the word Jahovah into the Address touched him very much. His emotions were easily aroused and he could barely respond with the tears swimming in his eyes. We see from the papers that Mrs Esther Hart and Miss Eva Hart are among the saved, but there is no mention of Mr Hart, and we fear the worst. Had he gone directly to Canada he would have been safely there by now, but he travelled via New York for the purpose of seeing a relative he had not seen for 30 years. Our hearts send out a wireless message of sympathy to the poor lady and child, deprived as we fear so untimely of their protector and probably of all this world's goods that they had with them, for Mr and Mrs Hart had gone out with a few pounds to start afresh in a new world at an age when most people are thinking of retiring from business.

On returning to Britain they lived with Esther's parents. They always maintained that *Titanic* had split in half, and this was proven when the ship was located in 1985. She died at Romford on 7 September 1928, aged sixty-five.

Eva put her vocal abilities to good use during her life, including becoming a professional singer in Australia, and she organised entertainment for troops during the Second World War. She stated categorically that she had seen *California* much closer to the scene of the disaster than has been accepted. She was awarded an MBE in 1974, and died at Chadwell Heath on Valentine's Day, 14 February 1996, aged ninety-one.

The house where the family lived is now a care home named Hart House, and a public house in Romford was named The Eva Hart in her honour. The letter that Esther and Eva wrote in the library on *Titanic* was sold at auction in 2014.

James Hart

James Hart was born at Didsbury in Manchester, during the latter half of 1858. He was the son of James Hart (born in Kent in 1823), who was a beer retailer, and his wife Maria (formerly Windus, born in Hampshire in 1829). They had married at St Thomas's Church in Winchester on 22 December 1851. James had three known older siblings: Maria, born in Manchester in 1853; Mary Ann, born in Manchester in 1854; and George, born in 1857. The 1861 census records the family living at Rusholme in Manchester.

He joined the Union Castle Line when it was established in 1900, and worked as a fireman or stoker on their vessels, which carried the Royal Mail, and therefore ran a strict timetable between Southampton and Cape Town in South Africa.

At the time of the 1911 census he is recorded as living as a lodger with a crane driver named Joseph Summers, and his wife and daughter, at 51 College Road in Southampton, being described as a ship's fireman. He was a member of the Seafarers' Union, and he had previously served on *Olympic*. He was to report for duty on *Titanic* on 6 April 1912. James Hart lost his life in the disaster, and if his body was recovered it was never identified.

His identity was mistaken to be that of a man called Thomas Hart, who was said to have also signed on *Titanic* as a fireman on 6 April 1912. However, the handwritten initial on the signing on papers was mistaken for a T, when it is obviously a J. The story was first reported in the *Liverpool Daily Post* that Thomas Hart, a native of Liverpool, went to the local pub to celebrate his new job on the night before boarding, where he drank heavily, apparently dozed off, and when he woke up his discharge book was gone. Following the theft he walked about Southampton for several days in a confused state, ashamed and disappointed in himself, until he finally returned home to his shocked mother in Liverpool. It was thought that another man signed on in his name and died in the disaster, but as no man named Thomas Hart signed on the ship is it likely that Tom's papers were discarded as useless by a thief or he just mislaid them.

There is an obituary notice in *The Southampton Daily Echo* for April 1913, where he is 'remembered by his mother'; and another obituary from his two sisters in the *Southampton Times and Hampshire Express* for April 1914, which states: 'In loving memory of James Hart, late of 51 College Street, Southampton, who lost his life on the ill-fated *Titanic*, April 15th 1912. Gone but not forgotten.'

In James Cameron's film an infamous game of cards (or chance) took place in which Leonardo DiCaprio gambled with his ship's papers. This scene is based on the Thomas Hart incident.

Wallace Henry Hartley

Wallace Hartley was born on 2 June 1878, at 92 Greenfield Road in Colne, Lancashire, the eldest son and second child of a mill manager named Albion Hartley (born at Colne in September 1850, died at Knaresborough in Yorkshire in March 1934), and his wife, Elizabeth (formerly Foulds, born circa 1850, died in Colne in September 1874).

He was educated at the George Street Wesleyan School, and was first introduced to music as a choirboy at the Bethel Independent Methodist Church, where his father was the bandmaster, and later he learnt to play the violin.

Wallace was aged fifteen when the family moved to a house named 'Surreyside' in West Park Street, Dewsbury, West Yorkshire, where he was soon giving solo violin performances.

On leaving school he gained employment as a bank clerk. He went on to lead orchestras in Harrogate and Bridlington, and he was a member of the Savage Club in Leeds.

Wallace began working for the music agency CW and FN Black of Liverpool, in 1909, which supplied musicians for Cunard and the White Star Line. He took up a position with Cunard entertaining passengers on cruises across the Atlantic on such liners as the *Mauretania* and *Lusitania*. By the time he became bandmaster on *Titanic* in 1912 he had made about eighty voyages.

Wallace was assigned to be the bandmaster for the RMS *Titanic*. He had proposed to Maria Robinson, and at first he was reluctant to leave her. However, he decided that working on the maiden voyage of *Titanic* would give him possible contacts for future work, and he was able to spend some time with her in her home town of Boston Spa the week before boarding the new ship.

All the members of the orchestra were employed by C W and F N Black, who had contracts with all of the steamer companies to provide musicians. They had accommodation in second class and they all boarded the liner at Southampton.

A newspaper at the time reported: 'The part played by the orchestra on board *Titanic* in her last dreadful moments will rank among the noblest in the annals of heroism at sea.'

Wallace's body was one of only three band members that were recovered by the *Mackay-Bennett* as number 224 on 4 May 1912, having been in the water for twenty days. He was described as having brown hair, and he was still wearing his uniform with green facings, a brown overcoat, black boots and green socks. The effects found on his body were a gold fountain pen bearing the initials W H H, a diamond solitaire ring, a silver cigarette case, a silver match box inscribed: 'W H H from Collinson's Staff, Leeds', a nickel watch, a gold chain, a gold cigar holder, a stud, a pair of scissors, some British and American coins, letters and a telegram to Hotley, Bandmaster 'Titanic'. It has been said that he had his music box strapped to his body.

His remains were embalmed and packed in ice, and transferred from Halifax to Boston, where they were placed on *Arabic*, which arrived in Liverpool on 12 May, then on to Colne.

About 4,000 people lined the route of the funeral procession on 18 May, as the rosewood casket led by seven bands made its way to the Bethel Independent Methodist Church. Over 1,000 people packed into the chapel that was only built to hold 700, and Wallace Hartley was laid to rest in what one newspaper called 'pageantry beyond belief' in Colne Cemetery. In 1915 a statue of Wallace was erected just to the side of the rectory on Albert Road, and the area around the statue has recently been renovated.

In the 1997 film *Titanic* he was portrayed by a Welsh actor named Jonathan Evans-Jones.

In April 2013 the letter Wallace wrote to his parents was sold at auction. Modern research suggests that his music bag containing his violin was sent back to Maria. It is believed to have been owned by someone in Lancashire when it came into the hands of an auctioneer in 2006, and after seven years of investigation it was proven to be authentic and was sold in October 2013.

Benjamin and Ellen Howard

Ben Howard was born on 10 May 1848, at 137 Cotton Street, Ashton-under-Lyne, Lancashire (now in Tameside, Greater Manchester), being baptised on 3 December that year. He was the youngest of six children to Joseph Howard (born at Glossop in 1801), and his second wife Ann (born at Saddleworth (then in Yorkshire) in 1814). His father was a cotton mill spinner, and all the family worked in the cotton industry. Joseph had first been married at Glossop in 1824, to a woman named Harriot (Brunt), and he had a daughter and a son from his first relationship. Ben had two older sisters and an older brother all born at Ashton-under-Lyne between 1836 and 1845.

His parents are believed to have died by the time of the 1861 census, and Ben was thirteen years old, working as a farmer's boy. He is recorded as a brother-in-law, residing with his sister Mary Ann and her husband, Samuel Kenworthy, a Saddleworth-born farmer of 14 acres of land, at Mill Barn, Saddleworth. Elizabeth and James were living with their Uncle John at Dukinfield in Cheshire.

The Great Western Railway reached Swindon in Wiltshire, in 1840, and the town was selected as a place to establish an engine building and maintenance works. There was no heavy industry in the area so workers had to be moved in from the rest of the country.

By 1871 Ben had moved to live at 4 Bridge Street in Swindon, and he is recorded as a brother-in-law, living at the home of his oldest sister, Sarah, and her husband, and he had gained employment as a bolt maker at the Swindon Railway Works.

By 1861 Ellen was living with her aunt Mary, and her husband, Henry Wheeler, at 21 Bridge Street in Swindon, stated as being a niece to the family. Ellen was still living with her aunt in 1871, although the census, if recorded correctly, states that they lived at 22 Bridge Street, Swindon.

On 16 May 1872, Ben married Ellen Truelove Arman, at St Michael's and All Angels Church in Highworth. Ellen had been born at Moredon, Rodbourne Cheney near Swindon, on 14 April 1851. Her mother is believed to have been Ann Arman, who was born at Chiseldon, and in 1851 was a servant visiting the home of her sister and her husband, Henry and Mary Wheeler, at Moredon.

By the time of the 1881 census they lived at 84 Cheltenham Street in Swindon, and Ben was still working as a bolt maker at the Railway Works. They had three children, William Henry (born in 1873), Frederick Charles (born in 1878), and Ethel Louise (born in 1879), who were all born in Swindon. They were apparently reasonably well off as they employed a servant.

By 1891 Ben had been promoted to assistant foreman bolt maker at the railway works, they had an addition to the family, Herbert Benjamin, born in Swindon on 16 February 1887, and they had a boarder. The family were residing at 85 Cheltenham Street in Swindon, which, if recorded correctly, was next door to their original house. In 1901 Ben had been promoted to foreman bolt maker at the Railway Works.

Herbert immigrated to Idaho in the United States prior to 1911, and Frederick decided to join him. Ben was retired when he and Ellen decided to cross the Atlantic to visit their sons. They paid £26 for tickets and boarded *Titanic* as second-class passengers, their destination being Idaho.

Sadly, Ben and Ellen never reached their destination and died in the disaster. If their bodies were recovered they were not identified.

Joseph Abraham Hyman

Joseph Hyman was a Russian Jew, born in about 1880, to Samuel Hyman (born in Russia in 1848) and his wife Leah (born in Poland on 15 September 1853). He had a brother named Henry and a sister named Etta, who became Mrs Rosenberg. He came to Britain as a young man and settled into Manchester's thriving Jewish community. He married his Manchester-born wife, Esther (formerly Levy), at Prestwich in 1902. It would seem that after their marriage they lived in Scotland, where some descendants are living to this day. By the time of the 1911 census they had five children: Julius was born in Glasgow in 1903; Annie was born in Glasgow in 1904; Lilian was born in Kilmarnock in 1906; and Morris was born in Glasgow in 1907. They moved to Manchester in about 1908, where Ena was born in 1909, and at that time they were living at 45 Stocks Street in Cheetham.

Abraham is remembered as a quiet man. He was stated to be aged thirty-four and was described as a framer living at 34 Lord Street in Cheetham Hill, Manchester, when he boarded *Titanic* as a third-class passenger going to America to join his brother Harry, who lived at 1369 North Street, Springfield, Massachusetts. He was aiming to set up a new life there, and his wife and family were going to join him once he had got established. He left a graphic account of the dreadful events that occurred as the disaster unfolded.

While he was recuperating in New York he noticed how the shops were aimed at the city's cosmopolitan population, and during his stay there he saw a delicatessen that specialised in Kosher food and decided to try to establish one when he returned to England. However, he was too scared to get back onto a ship, but his family were still back in Manchester, and after receiving news of the tragedy his wife refused to sail across the Atlantic, so the only way he could summon up the nerve to get back home was after his brother had got him drunk.

When he arrived back in Manchester he set up a small delicatessen at 230 Waterloo Road, Cheetham Hill, modelled on the one he had seen in New York, and named it J A Hyman Limited. Abraham's well-thumbed book containing traditional recipes such as curing salt beef and gefilte fish still exists. Word of his amazing escape from *Titanic* spread around the area, and he became a local celebrity where people would point and say: 'Look it's the man from Titanic.' It didn't take long for the shop to be known as 'Titanic's', which was incorporated into the name, and is still used by most of the customers of J A Hyman (Titanics) Limited to this day.

He and Esther had two more children, Jonas (born in 1913) and Rachel (born in 1915), and the family lived at the shop on Waterloo Road. Sadly, Esther died there on 14 September 1927, aged forty-six. He remarried on 9 June 1929, at the New Kahal Chassidim Synagogue. His new wife was also called Esther, a widow who lived a few doors away at 385 Waterloo Road. She was born at Cheetham in 1886, and her maiden name was Rosengrass. She had married a jeweller named Abraham Libbert in 1909, but he died in 1921. They had a son and daughter named Jack and Fanny; so Joseph was now the head of a family with seven children and two stepchildren.

They moved to Southport, where Esther died on 9 June 1951, aged sixty-five, so Joseph returned to Manchester, where he lived at 25 Crumpsall Lane in Crumpsall. He died at the Victoria Memorial Jewish Hospital on 6

March 1956, aged seventy-five, and he was buried in the North Manchester Jewish Cemetery in Blackley, Manchester.

The Hymans and the families of other victims attended a memorial event in Southampton on 10 April 2012, the centenary of the day *Titanic* left that town to begin its ill-fated journey. A descendant stated 'Joseph used to wake up every night screaming with nightmares that lasted for the rest of his life. Then, there were no psychiatrists or recognised conditions such as post-traumatic stress disorder.'

Violet Constance Jessop

Violet Jessop was born on 2 October 1887, in the Pampas near Bahia Blanca in Buenos Aires, Argentina, where her Roman Catholic parents had moved from Dublin to South America to take up sheep farming. Her parents were William Raymond Jessop, and his wife, Katherine (formerly Kelly). Violet was the first of nine children, six of whom survived. Violet contracted tuberculosis as a child, and doctors warned her parents that the illness was likely to be fatal, but she managed to pull through and survive what was then a dreaded killer disease. They moved to live at Mendoza, where William became the local stationmaster, and then a fuel inspector. He became ill with cancer in 1903 and died from complications arising from surgery, so the family returned to Britain.

Violet was stated to have 'grey-blue eyes, auburn hair, and spoke with an Irish accent'. Her mother found a job as a stewardess for the Royal Mail Line while Violet attended convent school. When her mother's health began to deteriorate, Violet had to give up her education and she too became a stewardess with the Royal Mail Line, joining the *Orinoco* in 1908, before transferring to the White Star Line. Apparently, she didn't want to work for the White Star Line at first because she didn't want to go on the North Atlantic run because of the adverse weather conditions, and she had been told that many of the passengers were very demanding. She worked long hours for low pay, and she was on board the *Olympic* when it collided with HMS *Hawke* in the Solent in 1911. However, she is said to have got to like that ship and she didn't really want to transfer to *Titanic*, but her friends persuaded her that it would be a 'wonderful experience', so Violet, 'dressed in a new ankle-length suit', set off in a horse-drawn cab from her home at 71 Shirley Road in Bedford Park, London, to join *Titanic*.

During the Great War she became a nurse with the British Red Cross, and was assigned to work on HMHS *Britannic*, which had been converted into a hospital ship for 3,000 patients. However, Nurse Jessop became involved in her third disaster when the vessel hit a mine as it crossed the Aegean Sea and sank within an hour, taking the lives of thirty people.

She stated 'I leaped into the water but was sucked under the ship's keel which struck my head. I escaped, but years later when I went to my doctors because of a lot of headaches he discovered I had once sustained a fracture of the skull.'

It was her opinion that the thickness of her auburn hair had probably cushioned the blow and saved her life.

She described the stricken *Britannic* as it went down:

> The white pride of the ocean's medical world … dipped her head a little, then a little lower and still lower. All the deck machinery fell into the sea like a child's toys. Then she took a fearful plunge, her stern rearing hundreds of feet into the air until with a final roar, she disappeared into the depths.

Fireman Jack Priest, who had been on *Olympic* and *Titanic* at the same time as Violet, described his escape from HMHS *Britannic*:

> … most of us jumped in the water but it was no good we was pulled right in under the blades … I shut my eyes and said goodbye to this world, but I was struck with a big piece of the boat and got pushed right under the blades and I was going around like a top … I came up under some of the wreckage … everything was going black to me when someone on top was struggling and pushed the wreckage away so I came up just in time before I was nearly done for … there was one poor fellow drowning and he caught hold of me but I had to shake him off so the poor fellow went under.

After the war, Violet continued to work for the White Star Line, before joining the Red Star Line and then returning to the Royal Mail Line. While employed with Red Star she went on two round-the-world cruises on the *Belgenland*, the company's largest ship.

She lived at 28 Burlington Road in Chiswick, and on 29 October 1923, which was a Monday, she married John James Lewis (born on 3 November 1876 in Liverpool, died in 1959), who also worked on ships, at Our Lady of Grace and St Edward Church on Chiswick High Road. However, the marriage was 'Brief and Disastrous', and lasted about a year. Violet's niece stated 'They just didn't get on'. She is said to have used her married name for legalities, but used her single name for every other purpose.

Violet retired from the sea in 1950 and bought a sixteenth-century thatched cottage called 'Maythorn' in the village of Great Ashfield, about 9 miles east of Bury St Edmunds in Suffolk. She is said to have filled her home with mementoes of her time at sea, and she owned a smallholding where she kept hens.

One stormy night during her retirement she said that she had a phone call from a woman who asked her if she saved a baby on the night that *Titanic* sank. 'Yes!' Violet replied, and the woman answered 'I was that baby'. Then she laughed, and hung up. Her friend and biographer, John Maxtone-Graham, suggested that it was most likely someone in the village playing a prank on her, to which she replied 'No, John, I had never told that story to anyone before I told you now'.

Violet was in her eighty-fourth year when she developed bronchial pneumonia and died of congestive heart failure at St Mary's Hospital in Bury St Edmunds on 5 May 1971. She was buried next to her sister, Eileen (Meehan) in the cemetery in the nearby village of Hartest. Her weather-worn gravestone states: 'Violet Constance Jessop, beloved sister, who died 5th May 1971 in her 84th year, fortified by rites of Holy Mother Church. On her soul sweet Jesus have mercy.'

Charles John Joughin

Charles Joughin was born at 1 Patten Street in Birkenhead, on 3 August 1878. He was the son of a licensed victualler named John Edwin Joughin (born in Liverpool in 1846, died in 1886), and his wife Ellen (formerly Crombleholm, born in Birkenhead in 1850, died in 1938). He married in Liverpool in 1907, and had a daughter named Agnes Lilian.

He transferred from *Olympic*, and was on board *Titanic* for her delivery trip from Belfast to Southampton. When he signed on again, as chief baker, in Southampton on 4 April 1912, he gave his address as Elmhurst, Leighton Road in Southampton.

According to his obituary, he was on the SS *Oregon* when it sank in Boston Harbour. He also served on ships operated by the American Export Lines, as well as on Second World War troop transports.

His second wife, Nellie Ripley, died in 1943, and Charles died at the Barnert Memorial Hospital in New Jersey, on 9 December 1956, aged seventy-eight, leaving a daughter, Agnes Joughin, of Liverpool, and a step-daughter, Mrs Henry (Rose) Stoehr, of Paterson. He was buried at the Cedar Lawn Cemetery in New Jersey. In the 1997 film *Titanic* he was portrayed by a Dubliner named Liam Tuohy.

Henry Forbes Julian

Henry Julian was born in Cork in Ireland on 9 May 1861, the oldest of three sons in the family of six children of a coach builder named Henry Julian (born in Bristol in 1827), and his wife, Marie (formerly Neligan, born in Cork in 1836), the daughter of an Irish officer who had served throughout the Peninsula War with 'conspicuous heroism', and had taken part in the siege of Badajoz in 1812. Henry began his education in Cork.

By 1869 his father had moved his coach building business to the industrial heartland of Bolton, where Henry continued his education, and by 1881 they were living at 8 Back of the Bank in the district of Little Bolton. Henry went on to study chemistry at Owens College in Manchester, as a pupil of Sir Henry Roscoe. He completed his education in South Kensington.

In October 1886 he went to Natal in South Africa, where he gained employment as a metallurgist and analyst. He eventually became a mine manager and consulting engineer in the gold mining regions of Natal, Barberton, Johannesburg and Kimberley. He remained in South Africa for seven years, during which time he invented and recorded the patent for the Electrical Chemical Gold and Silver Extracting Apparatus. To market the device Henry set up a limited company of which he was the managing director and major shareholder.

He moved to live at Frankfurt in Germany in 1893, where he worked as a technical adviser on mining and metallurgy to the Deutsche Gold and Silver Scheide Anstalt Company. At this time he co-wrote *Cyaniding Gold and Silver Ores*. His work ensured that he was well travelled, having crossed the Atlantic Ocean thirteen times, with destinations such as Mexico, the West Indies, the United States and Canada, and he toured Eastern Europe extensively.

Henry came back to England in 1895, where he settled in the West Country. He rented Ness House at Shaldon near the mouth of the River Teign in South Devon, with panoramic views of the sea and the town of Teignmouth. He also kept a residence in London. His interests were varied, and he was a founder member of the Royal Automobile Club and a member of the committee of the British Association. He joined the committee of the Torquay Natural History Society, and became an active member of the Devonshire Association, both founded by William Pengelly FRS FGS, the well-respected geologist.

His unmarried daughter, Hester, was also a member and soon she and Henry became a couple. They were married on 30 October 1902, at St Mary Magdelene Church at Upton in Torquay, and they made their home at a house called 'Redholme' in Braddon's Hill Road East in Torquay.

With several business interests and commitments Henry had to attend a meeting in San Francisco and he boarded the ship on the morning of 10 April. He lost his life in the disaster, and if his body was recovered it was never identified.

Just prior to his departure from Torquay his sister-in-law, Mrs Lydia Maxwell had asked him if he would prefer the new vessel, to which he replied 'Not in the least. I do not care at all for palm court and gymnasium and such extra attraction, and never visited them on *Mauretania*. I shall keep to the smoking room and library, and only just look over the vessel before starting.'

He left Torquay by train at 1.35 pm on 9 April. His wife, Hester, had been unable to travel because she was suffering with a bout of flu. He arrived at the South Western Hotel in Southampton about seven hours later, telling his wife that it was better she had not accompanied him because the weather was very cold with a strong wind.

He embarked on *Titanic* on the morning of 10 April, and made his way to the stern of the ship and to the starboard side, where he described his cabin as 'more like a small bedroom than a ship's cabin'. After his scheduled tour of the ship he wrote to his wife and mentioned the Cafe Parisien and the gymnasium, which he said was 'full of the most wonderful machines'. The last his wife heard from him was on 11 April when he stated that he was most comfortable, and he had slept well, the ship being so steady. He also mentioned that he had met his old friend, Colonel John Weir in board. In 1914 an impressive memorial tablet was unveiled at the Church of St Mary

Magdalene, to provide a lasting tribute to him, and his name is commemorated at his wife's grave in Torquay Cemetery.

Charles Herbert Lightoller *DSC and Bar*

Charles Lightoller lived a most eventful and adventurous life. He was born at Chorley in Lancashire, on 30 March 1874, the youngest of seven children to Frederick James Lightoller (born in Chorley on 6 January 1842, committed suicide at Waipawa in New Zealand on 12 December 1913), and his wife, Sarah Jane (formerly Widdows, born at Leigh on 30 October 1843), who had married at Blackpool in 1863. Having already lost a child named James at birth, Sarah died of scarlet fever soon after Charles was born, followed by two of his siblings, Richard and Caroline. He had surviving sisters named Jane, Gertrude and Ethel.

The Lightoller family was involved in the cotton spinning industry and the Lightoller Mill on Standish Street was very well known in the town. Frederick gave up his life as a captain in the army to take over his father's cotton mills. They lived at 'The Firs' in Yarrow, Chorley, which was one of the first houses to have electric lighting in the town.

His father married Margaret Barton at Chorley on 6 January 1876. Their marriage was childless, and Margaret died on 19 September 1881. Fred had an affair with the family maid, Joyce Gladwin, resulting in the birth of a daughter named Janet in 1883. Fred, Jane, Joyce and Janet moved to New Zealand, leaving Charles, Gertrude and Ethel with family in England, although Fred remained in contact with them.

Charles attended the Chorley Grammar School. He was said to be a bright boy with great potential, but he was apparently difficult to manage, and when he was thirteen he asked if he could go to sea.

In February 1888 he became apprenticed to the William Price Line of Liverpool, and was soon aboard the *Primrose Hill*, a large sailing ship, bound around Cape Horn for San Francisco. His next voyage was on the *Holt Hill*. She lost her mast in a storm in the South Atlantic and was forced to put into Rio de Janeiro during a revolution and a smallpox epidemic. After makeshift repairs, she lost her new mast in another storm in the Indian Ocean and on 13 November 1889 ran aground on St Paul, an uninhabited island in the Indian Ocean. The chief mate was killed in the shipwreck, and after eight days the survivors were rescued by the *Coorong* and taken to Adelaide in Australia, where they spent Christmas 1889.

Charles signed on with the clipper ship *Duke of Abercorn* for his return to England. His third voyage was again on the *Primrose Hill,* this time to Calcutta in India. On this voyage they survived a cyclone. In Calcutta, Charles passed his Second Mate's Certificate. While serving as third mate on the windjammer *Knight of St Michael* the cargo of coal caught fire. For his successful efforts in fighting the fire and saving the ship, Charles was promoted to second mate.

He obtained his Mate's ticket. He left the windjammers and joined Elder Dempster's African Royal Mail Service, starting a career on steamships. After three years on the West African Coast, he nearly died from a heavy bout of malaria.

Charles went to Canada in 1898 to prospect for gold in the Klondike Gold Rush in Yukon, and he had a brief stint as a cowboy in Alberta. He worked his passage back as a cattle wrangler on a cattle boat, and arrived back in England penniless in 1899. He obtained his master's certificate and joined Greenshields and Cowie, where he made another trip on a cattle boat, this time as third mate of the *Knight Companion.*

He joined the White Star Line in January 1900, and his first assignment was as fourth officer on *Medic,* a passenger-cargo liner on the Britain-South Africa-Australia run. After one voyage, he was switched to the Atlantic routes, mostly on *Majestic*, his first employment under Captain Edward Smith.

While travelling to Australia on *Medic* he met Iowa Sylvania Zillah Hawley-Wilson, a seventeen-year-old Australian known as Sylvia, who was returning home to Hell's Hole in Sydney after a year of education in England. They became a couple and were married at St James's Church in Sydney on 15 December 1903. At the time of the disaster they were living in a residence at Hound in Netley Abbey near Southampton.

In 1907 he was promoted to third officer on *Oceanic,* and in the same year the home port of the *Oceanic* was changed from Liverpool to Southampton, which meant another move for the Lightoller family. From second officer on *Oceanic,* Lightoller moved up to first on the *Majestic,* and then moved back to *Oceanic* as its first officer.

Charles boarded *Titanic* just two weeks before her maiden voyage, and sailed as first officer for the sea trials. Just before *Titanic* sailed, Captain Smith made Henry Wilde his chief officer, which caused the original chief officer, William Murdoch, to have to step down to first officer, while Charles was dropped to second officer, and the original second officer, David Blair, was forced to stand down. As *Titanic* left Southampton, Henry and Charles were stationed on the forecastle supervising the boatswains dealing with hawsers.

Charles was rescued in collapsible B dinghy, which included Algernon Barkworth, Harold Bride and Charles Joughin.

Charles was called to testify at the American and British Inquiries into the disaster. As the most senior surviving officer, he found himself having to defend the captain, the officers and the company against some of the more serious charges brought against them. Charles returned to sea in 1913 as first officer of *Oceanic.*

During the Great War, *Oceanic* was commissioned as an armed merchant cruiser on the Northern Patrol, and Charles became Lieutenant Lightoller of the Royal Navy. *Oceanic's* job was to patrol a 150-mile stretch of water in the area of the Shetland Islands. She ran aground near the island of Foula, and three weeks later *Oceanic* broke up in a storm and was gone.

Charles's next assignment was to *Campania,* a Cunard liner converted to a seaplane carrier. 'Lights' now found himself as the observer in a Short 184 seaplane. In June 1915, during a Grand Fleet exercise off Iceland, he was the observer on the only plane able to get into the air. They located the Blue Fleet, and for the first time in history, a plane sent up by a fleet at sea succeeded in locating an enemy fleet. Just before Christmas 1915, Lightoller got his own command, the torpedo boat HMTB *117.* During his tour with this boat, on 31 July 1916, Lightoller attacked the Zeppelin L31 with the ship's Hotchkiss guns. For his actions Lightoller was awarded the Distinguished Service Cross and he was also promoted to commander of the torpedo boat destroyer *Falcon.* On 14 April 1918, Lightoller was again off watch, lying in his bunk, when *Falcon* collided with the trawler *John Fitzgerald.* She stayed afloat for a few hours, eventually sinking just about the same time, six years to the day after *Titanic* sinking.

Lightoller was now given a new command, the destroyer *Garry.* On 19 July 1918, they rammed and sank the German submarine *UB-110.* The ramming damaged the bows of the *Garry* so badly that she had to steam 100 miles in reverse to relieve the strain on the forward bulkheads as she returned to port for repairs. For this action Lightoller was awarded a bar to his DSC and promoted to lieutenant commander.

During the war, Sylvia Lightoller became well known for keeping an open house to ANZAC troops when they lived at the Cottage in Cockfosters.

At the end of 1918, Lightoller came out of the Royal Navy as a full commander. On his return to White Star he was appointed chief officer of the *Celtic*, having been passed over for a position on the *Olympic*. The new management wanted to forget *Titanic* and all those associated with her; none of the surviving officers from *Titanic* ever got their own commands. However, Charles was not interested in remaining chief officer of the *Celtic* indefinitely, so, after well over twenty years of service, he resigned from White Star Line.

The Lightollers opened a guest house and after a few years had some minor success in property speculation. They purchased a discarded Admiralty steam launch in 1929, and had her refitted and lengthened, converting her into a diesel motor yacht that was christened *Sundowner* by his wife. Throughout the 1930s she was used by the Lightoller family, mainly for trips around England and Europe. In 1935 he published *ZTitanic and Other Ships*, and on 1 November 1936 he recited his account for the BBC radio programme *I Was There*.

In July 1939, Charles and Sylvia were asked by the Royal Navy to perform a survey of the German coastline. This they did under the guise of an elderly couple on vacation in their yacht. When the Second World War broke out in 1939, the Lightollers were raising chickens in Hertfordshire. Their youngest son, Brian, was a pilot in the RAF, and on the first night of hostilities he was killed in a bombing raid on Wilhelmshaven. On 31 May 1940, Charles got a phone call from the Admiralty asking him to take the *Sundowner* to Ramsgate, where a Navy crew would take over and sail her to Dunkirk. Lightoller informed them that nobody would take the *Sundowner* to Dunkirk but him.

On 1 June 1940, the sixty-six-year old Lightoller, accompanied by his eldest son Roger and an eighteen-year-old sea scout named Gerald, took the *Sundowner* and sailed from Ramsgate for Dunkirk and the trapped British Expeditionary Force. Although the *Sundowner* had never carried more than twenty-one people before, they succeeded in carrying a total of 130 men from the beaches of Dunkirk. In addition to the three crew members, there were two crew members who had been rescued from another small boat, the motor cruiser *Westerly*. There were another three naval ratings also rescued from waters off Dunkirk, plus 122 troops taken from the destroyer *Worcester*. Despite numerous bombing and strafing runs by Luftwaffe aircraft, they all arrived safely back to Ramsgate just about twelve hours after they had departed.

It is said that when one of the soldiers heard that the captain had been on *Titanic*, he was tempted to jump overboard. However his mate was quick to reply that if Lightoller could survive *Titanic*, he could survive anything and that was all the more reason to stay.

Commander Lightoller joined the Home Guard, but the Royal Navy engaged him to work with the Small Vessel Pool until the end of the war. Their eldest son, Roger, had joined the Royal Navy, where he commanded motor gunboats. During the last months of the war, he was killed during a German Commando raid on Granville on the north French coast.

After the war, Lights went into the boat building business, first with an outside partner, then with his son, Trevor. *Sundowner* was retrieved and refurbished, and their company, Richmond Slipways, located at 1 Duck's Walk, near Richmond Bridge, specialised in police river launches. Charles and Sylvia lived over their place of work.

Charles died of heart disease on 8 December 1952, aged seventy-eight. He was cremated at Mortlake Crematorium and his ashes were scattered in the Garden of Remembrance. It is possible that he may have succumbed prematurely to his illness. A life-long pipe smoker and suffering from heart disease, he was living in London in the midst of that city's great smog of 1952 when he died from complications of his illness.

Louise Patten, the finance businesswoman and author, is his granddaughter. Charles was depicted by a thirty-four-year-old Londoner named Jonathan Phillips in the 1997 film *Titanic*.

David Livshin

David Lifschitz was of an Ashkenazi Jewish background, born in the Baltic Sea port of Leipaja, Kurzeme in Latvia, who gave his age as twenty-five (born in about 1887) and is believed to have served in the Russian Army. He anglicised his name to Livshin, and had been in England for about a year, living at 36 Strong Street in Lower Broughton, Salford. He was a jeweller, and on moving to Manchester he had started a watch-making business at Strangeways. In 1912 he married a twenty-year-old Russian girl named Chyna Hodes, and decided to emigrate to Montreal in Canada to join his sisters and send for his wife later. Chyna was expecting their first child.

His original intention was to travel to north America on a ship called the *Grampian*, but on realising that in 1912 the important celebration of the Jewish feast of the Passover was from 2 to10 April, it seems that he preferred to spend the holiday at home with his wife and managed to exchange his ticket with a man called Abraham Harmer, who was scheduled to sail on *Titanic*.

He boarded *Titanic* at Southampton under his assumed name as a third-class passenger. According to Captain Rostron, 'Mr Harmer' was one of the four people buried at sea from the *Carpathia*. He may have been the fourth person picked up by lifeboat 14, or the 'lifeless body', referred to by Charles Lightoller, transferred from Collapsible B to lifeboat 12 during the night. Algernon Barkworth also talked about a dead body being transferred.

Chyna gave birth on 3 September 1912, and named her son after his father. She applied to the Liverpool Relief Fund for assistance, and was granted a monthly payment but requested that she be given a reduced sum and an immediate cash payment in order that she might return to Russia to take young David to visit his grandparents. She was still in Russia when the Great War broke out and was unable to leave. The family endured severe deprivations during this time and it was not until 1920 that they were able to return to Manchester.

David Livshin junior became a highly respected member of the medical profession. He was married in 1948, having a son and two daughters, and he died in Manchester in 1992.

Harold Godfrey Lowe

Harold Lowe was born at Eglwys Rhos, Llanrhos in Caernarfonshire (now Conwy County), on 21 November 1882. He was the fourth of eight children born to George and Harriet Lowe. He lived in Barmouth, where he was educated, and at the age of fourteen his parents wanted him to start an apprenticeship with a successful businessman in Liverpool, but Harold decided that he '... was not going to work for anybody for nothing ... I wanted to be paid for my labour,' so he ran away and joined a ship in which he spent five years serving along the West African coast.

He joined the White Star Line only fifteen months before sailing on *Titanic*, serving as third officer on *Tropic* and *Belgic*.

On his return home to Barmouth after the disaster, 1,300 people attended a reception in his honour, held at the Picture Pavilion, and he was presented with a commemorative gold watch and chain bearing the inscription:

'Presented to Harold Godfrey Lowe, 5th Officer, RMS Titanic, by his friends in Barmouth and elsewhere, in recognition and appreciation of his gallant services at the foundering of Titanic, 15 April 1912.' It was reported 'Mr Lowe was so overcome by his feelings at this mark of esteem on the part of his Barmouth friends that he was only able to express his feelings in a single sentence'.

By September 1912 he was in Australia as third officer on *Medic* where it was reported 'For various reasons, one of which is that he is "so sick of it all" and desires, if possible, to forget about the past. Mr Lowe is disinclined to discuss the tragedy.'

Harold married Ellen Marian (formerly Whitehouse) in September 1913. They had two children named Florence Josephine Edge 'Josie', and Harold William George.

During the Great War he was a commander in the Royal Naval Reserve, and saw service in Vladivostok during the Russian Revolution and Civil War of 1919; attaining the rank of lieutenant RNR.

After the war he returned to service with international Mercantile Marine ships and the White Star Line.

In 1931 he retired to live in a large house on Marine Crescent at the waterfront overlooking the River Conway at Deganwy, where he came to be known as 'Titanic Lowe'. He served as a 'high-profile' Conway town councillor.

In 1936 a young girl named Annette Roberts visited the Lowe's for afternoon tea. She had been instructed to call him Commander, but found him to be a 'jovial man'. She recalled 'the huge table set for tea, with a dainty brass shovel and brush for clearing away the crumbs'.

Apparently, Commander Lowe thought it was hugely funny to secrete a whoopee cushion under the covering of Annette's chair at the table, and when she sat down she was 'ashamed and embarrassed when a loud noise emanated from beneath her'.

> I remember Mr Lowe as full of fun, there was a lot of laughter and jokes thrown around that afternoon. I only listened to the conversation because children really did only speak when spoken to in those days. I remember it was a very dainty afternoon tea with sandwiches and scones, it was quite grand. *Titanic* wasn't mentioned that afternoon, but I do know Mr Lowe had been a very brave man that night.

During the Second World War he volunteered his home as a sector post and served as an air raid warden until ill health forced him into a wheelchair.

Harold died of hypertension at Deganwy on 12 May 1944, aged sixty-one, and he was buried in Llandrillo Yn Rhos Churchyard at Rhos-on-Sea, Colwyn Bay.

On 22 April 2012, a service of commemoration was held at the church, attended by his great nephew, John Harold Lowe, who lived in his old house at Deganwy, and several local dignitaries. Due to the determination of a local schoolgirl, a slate plaque has been placed in the harbour master's office at Barmouth, and a blue commemoration plaque at his former home in Deganwy. John stated that 'He was very reticent to talk about it. He talked to his son, my uncle about it, but I was forbidden to talk about it.'

Evelyn Marsden

Evelyn was born on 15 October 1883, at Stockyard Creek Railway Station, where her father, William Henry Marsden, was the master. Her mother was named Annie (formerly Bradshaw). Stockyard Creek is about 50 miles north of Adelaide, in the northern region of South Australia.

William later became stationmaster at Hoyleton, about 15 miles further north, and growing up in rural South Australia, Evelyn became an accomplished horsewoman. She spent holidays on a farm at Murray Bridge, where she was taught to row on the Murray River, even fighting her way against the tide.

She trained to be a nurse at the Royal Adelaide Hospital before choosing a life at sea with the famous White Star line. She was serving on the *Olympic* when it collided with HMS *Hawke*, and she joined *Titanic* as nurse/stewardess, looking after the first-class saloon passengers.

After *Titanic* hit the iceberg, Evelyn and a fellow stewardess were comforted by Assistant Surgeon John Simpson, who had also transferred from the *Olympic*. He took them to his cabin and gave them whiskey and water to calm their nerves. They didn't see him again; he was among those lost.

As passengers and crew abandoned ship, the skill Evelyn had gained on the Murray River was suddenly of vital importance. She helped row lifeboat number 16 until they were rescued the following morning. It was said that she also tended a baby.

Back in Hoyleton, Mr and Mrs Marsden spent several stressful days waiting for news of their daughter. Finally they received a two-word telegram, which told them all they needed to know: 'Safe. Evelyn.'

Soon after the disaster, Evelyn married her fiancé, ship's doctor William Abel James. He originally came from Monmouth in Wales and had settled in Australia in 1911; they had met aboard the *Olympic*. Later that year they arrived back in Australia aboard the SS *Irishman*. Evelyn went back to the Murray Bridge farm to thank her old friends for teaching her how to row.

The couple settled at 85 Curlewis Street in Bondi, where William became a general practitioner. During the Great War he served in Egypt as a doctor with the Australian Imperial Forces. There were no children from the marriage.

Evelyn died on 30 August 1938, aged fifty-four. William passed away just a week later, aged fifty-eight. They lie together at Waverley cemetery in Sydney. A headstone was erected on 5 October 2000.

Marian Meanwell

Mary Ann Ogden was born at Ramsbottom in Lancashire, on 7 December 1848, and she was baptised at Manchester Cathedral on 24 March 1850. She was the daughter of John Henry Ogden (born in 1825), a professor of music, and his wife, Ann (formerly Armstrong, born in 1825), who had married at Prestwich in Manchester on 17 September 1849. At the time of the 1861 census she and her mother were living as lodgers in Chorlton-on-Medlock in Manchester. She later used the name Marian. Some sources state that she spelled it as 'Marion', but as her original name is Mary Ann, it is more likely she used the former.

The family moved to Bradford in Yorkshire, where Mary took on a post as a milliner as soon as she was old enough to work. In 1868 she married a draper's assistant named Thomas Hilton Meanwell (born in Coningsby in Lincolnshire in 1849), and they settled at 10a Tempest Place in the Manningham district of Bradford. Nine months later she gave birth to Walter, and twin daughters, Margaret Ann and Annie Elizabeth, were born on 18 July 1872. However, Annie died a few weeks before her second birthday.

By the time of the 1881 census it seems that the couple had separated and Thomas had moved out of the family home and gone back to Lincolnshire, while Marian and Margaret were living at 7 Crapstan Street in Bradford.

Walter was taken to live with his paternal grandparents, John and Sarah, at Tattersall in Lincolnshire.

Thomas lived with Mary Jane Forman in Lincolnshire. They had three children and settled in Manchester. They eventually married in 1918, and Thomas died in the following year. Walter also returned to Manchester, becoming a greengrocer in Chorlton-on-Medlock, where he died in 1920.

Marian continued to work as a milliner and dressmaker, and moved to London, where she appears in the 1901 census as living at number 473 King's Road in Chelsea. A decade later she lived on her own at 60 Walterton Road in Paddington. However, it seems she had formed a relationship with a man named Edward Eli Costin, who was to receive her effects.

She told her cousin, Mrs Beck, who lived at Cambridge Street in Millom (now in Cumbria), she could write to her at 100 Lexington Avenue, New York, where she would be staying with Margaret.

She was due to take the ship *Majestic*, and on 4 April 1912, she stopped off in Liverpool to collect a baggage insurance ticket, number 1716, from White Star Line's offices. She then boarded the train to Eastbourne, where she stayed prior to embarking. On her arrival at Southampton she was told *Majestic* was unable to sail, and she would have to travel instead on *Titanic.*

Marian Meanwell died in the disaster, and if her body was recovered it was not identified. Margaret received $500 from Titanic Relief Fund the year after the tragedy, and a total of $350 from other American relief funds.

Marian's alligator-skin handbag with her purse and sodden boarding card still inside was salvaged from the wreckage and formed part of Titanic Exhibition. Some of her descendants were able to see the artefacts when the exhibition was in Manchester in 2005.

Michel Navratil

Michel Navratil was born on 13 August 1880, at Sered in Hungary, which in 1920 was renamed Szered, as part of Czechoslovakia, and is now in Slovakia. He was the son of Michal Navratil and his wife, Magdalena Navratilova. He later moved to Nice in France, where he began trading as a ladies' tailor.

He met Marcelle Mariana, daughter of Segundo Caretto, and his wife, Angela (formerly Bruno). Marcelle had been born at Buenos Aires in Argentina, on 31 January 1890, before moving to Nice via Genoa. They married in Westminster in London on 26 May 1907. They had two sons; Michel

Marcel, known as Lolo, who was born in Nice on 12 June 1908, and Edmond Roger, known as Momon, who was born in Lorraine on 5 March 1910.

However, by 1912 the business was in trouble, Michel was said to be very jealous and accused Marcelle of having an affair. Eventually she was forced to file for a divorce. She was given custody of the boys, but Michel was allowed to see them once a month. However, when her godfather left them with Michel for the Easter weekend of 1912, he did not know that Michel had made plans to take them with him to America. After stopping at Monte Carlo, he took them to London, where they stayed at the Charing Cross Hotel, before boarding *Titanic* as second-class passengers on 10 April 1912.

He wrote a letter to his mother in Hungary asking if his sister and her husband would be able to care for the boys, presumably if they were not allowed to stay in America.

On learning that the ship was in distress, it is said that Michel and some other passengers dressed the boys as best they could and took them up to the boat deck; other sources say they had just blankets wrapped around them. When Second Officer Lightoller ordered a locked-arm circle of crew members around collapsible D so that only women and children could get through, Michel handed the boys through them, stating to his elder son 'My child, when your mother comes for you, as she surely will, tell her that I loved her dearly, and still do. Tell her I expected her to follow us, so that we might all live happily together in the peace and freedom of the New World.'

Michel perished in the disaster, and his was body number 15 picked up by the *Mackay-Bennett*. He was described as having black hair and moustache, wearing a grey overcoat with green lining over a brown suit. Among his possessions was a loaded revolver. Because he had used a Jewish name, he was buried in the Baron de Hirsch Cemetery in Halifax, Nova Scotia, which was designated for Jewish victims.

The two boys were lowered into collapsible boat D, the last vessel to be launched from the stricken ship successfully, where Margaret Bechstein Hays wrapped the pair up in a large waterproof cape, in which she was also carrying her pet dog Bebe that she had bought in Paris. The two boys knew only their nicknames of Lolo and Momon, and just answered 'oui!' to everything they were asked, so on being rescued by the *Carpathia*, she and her husband, Frank, kept them at their large home at 304 West 83rd Street,

New York. During their stay with the couple it was reported 'They seem not the least bit homesick … and they are having the time of their lives'. Margaret received over 100 letters from people offering to adopt them.

Marcelle read of the two little French 'Titanic Orphans' who had been rescued. She wrote to Mrs Hays and asked for a photograph to be taken of the boys so she could identify them as her sons. On seeing the pictures, she confirmed that they were her boys and she contacted the White Star Line, who paid for her voyage to New York aboard the *Oceanic*. Described as 'a handsome widow of 24 … clad in deep mourning, with dark complexion and lustrous eyes', she recovered her children at the rooms of the Children's Society on 16 May. The Children's Society supported them during their stay in New York, and they returned to Nice aboard *Olympic*.

Edmond eventually married, and worked as an interior decorator and then he became an architect and builder. During the Second World War he fought with the French Army, was captured and made a prisoner-of-war. He managed to escape, but his health had suffered and he died in 1953. Marcelle died in 1974.

Michel attended college, and in 1933 he married a fellow student. He became a respected philosopher, and was honorary professor of psychology at the University of Montpellier.

He travelled to Wilmington in Delaware in 1987 to mark the seventy-fifth anniversary of the disaster. In the following year he joined ten fellow survivors at *Titanic* Historical Society Convention held in Boston, Massachusetts. In August 1996 he joined Eleanor Shuman and Edith Brown, two fellow survivors, on a cruise to the location of the wreck, where attempts were made to bring a large portion of the hull to the surface. During the trip he visited his father's grave for the only time.

Michel died in Montpellier on 30 January 2001, in his ninety-third year, as the last surviving male victim of *Titanic* disaster.

His daughter, Elisabeth, became an opera director. In 1982 she wrote a book about the experiences of her father, grandfather and uncle, the title in English being: *The Children of Titanic*, which was entitled *Survivors – A True-Life Titanic Story* when it went on sale in the United Kingdom.

Alice Frances Louisa Phillips

Alice Phillips was born at 85 High Street in Ilfracombe, Devon, on 26 January 1891. She was the only child of Escott Robert Phillips and his wife,

Hannah Marie (formerly Knight, born in Cardiff in 1868). Escott was the son of a police officer, and he had been born in Cardiff on 24 November 1868.

Having moved to live at Ilfracombe, Escott and Hannah married in 1890, and Escott gained employment as a porter at the Royal Clarence Hotel, before working in a local fishmonger's shop named T D Harding. A decade later they lived at 9 Belvedere, and in 1904 Hannah took over a boarding house in Westbourne Grove.

Sadly, Hannah was struck down with tuberculosis and died in August 1911. Alice's Uncle William had moved to the United States in 1892 to work as a painter, and lived with his wife and daughter at 700 13th Street in New Brighton near Pittsburgh, so, Escott having secured a position in Pittsburgh as a factory foreman, he and Hannah made the necessary plans to go to America.

They sold the house and stayed for a short while at the Central Hotel in Ilfracombe, before getting on the train on 9 April to travel the nine-hour journey to Southampton. They were due to board the American Lines ship *Philadelphia*, but the ongoing coal strike forced the cancellation of that ship and they were transferred to *Titanic*. That evening they walked down to Berth 44 where *Titanic* was being prepared for the journey, and afterwards Alice wrote to her grandmother, Charlotte in Ilfracombe: 'Dad and I have been to look at *Titanic*. It is a monstrous great boat as high as the Clarence Hotel, and I cannot tell you how long! We are going to embark tomorrow morning soon after breakfast.'

During the voyage Alice shared a cabin with Agnes Davis and her son, John, and Maude Sincock, all of whom lived at St Ives in Cornwall; and they shared their table at mealtimes with a family of four (possibly the Samuel Herman family).

As a result of her ordeal during the sinking, Alice became ill, but recovered sufficiently to train as a stenographer at her uncle's workplace. She received $650 from various American relief sources. However, she soon became homesick and decided to return to England; arriving in Liverpool on the *Baltic* on 2 November.

She eventually moved to Manchester. She met Henry Leslie Mead, an accounts clerk, who had been born on 23 June 1892, in Dublin, and was raised in Droylesden, Manchester. They married at St Mark's Church in Cheetham, on 5 February 1916. A daughter named Josephine was born in 1921.

It seems they lived in Salford, where Alice was struck down with influenza and died during the second quarter of 1923, aged just thirty-one. Josephine died a few months later.

Henry remarried in the following year, and raised a family. He died in Southport in 1977, aged eighty-four.

Kate Florence Phillips

Kate Phillips was born at King's Norton in Worcestershire (now a district of the City of Birmingham) on 1 January 1893. She was the third girl of four in the family of five children born between 1884 and 1899 to an engine fitter named Thomas Charles Phillips (born in Worcester in 1862) and his wife, Mary (formerly Smith, born in Worcester in 1861). They had married in Worcester in 1883.

In 1901 they were living in Martley Road in the parish of North Hallow, beside the River Severn near Worcester, and a decade later they lived at 34 Waterworks Road in Worcester, where Kate was described as a confectionary shop assistant.

Her companion, Henry, lost his life in the disaster and if his body was recovered it was never identified. Kate spent some time in New York being looked after by the Red Cross and on realising that a child had been conceived during the journey across the Atlantic, she returned home to Waterworks Road, where Ellen Mary was born on 11 January 1913.

The horrors of *Titanic* disaster almost certainly disturbed Kate's mind, and her family stated that she was never the same afterwards. She moved to London and worked as a shoe and hat salesperson, leaving Ellen in the care of her parents. She is said to have never spoken about Henry, and she married a cafe owner named Fred Watson in Hendon in 1918.

She took over the guardianship of Ellen in 1922, at about the time when Ellen was made aware that Henry Morley was her father, but their relationship was strained to the point where Kate's treatment of her daughter had to be investigated by the authorities. She became more unstable as she struggled through life, and at one time she was admitted to an asylum for her own protection after she drank an acid solution that was so strong that it burned the lining off her stomach. She was bedridden during the last years of her life, and having been abandoned by her husband, she died in Hendon on 27 March 1964, aged seventy-one. Having become estranged from Kate, Ellen did not attend her funeral because she had no idea that her mother had died.

Ellen, who was known as Betty, married a bus driver named Lawrence Farmer in 1935, and had a son named Robert. She was soon widowed, and as the country was at war she worked as a railway porter and married Frederick Walker in 1944. Not knowing her father was a deep disappointment to her, and she tried for many years to have his name included on her birth certificate, but without success. She died in her native Worcester in 1965, aged ninety-two.

Kate's pendant and trunk keys were included in the display organised aboard as part of the twentieth anniversary celebrations of the film *Titanic* held in Belfast in 2017, but her brown leather purse remains with the family. It is believed that the tragic love story of Henry and Kate and the pendant, known as 'Love of the Sea', were the inspiration for the Heart of the Ocean storyline between Rose (Kate Winslet) and Jack (Leonardo DiCaprio) in James Cameron's film.

Adolphe Saalfeld

Adolphe Saalfeld originally hailed from Oranienbaum, Anholt, in Germany, where he was born in 1865. He was the son of a Jew named Heinemann Salomon 'Henry' Saalfeld and his wife, Rosalie.

He moved to London in the 1880s, and in 1888 in Marylebone he married his 'dear wifey' Gertrude (formerly Harris) who came from Exeter. The 1891 census records them as living at 65 Sutherland Avenue in Paddington, London, where Adolphe was described as a clerk.

A decade later he had moved to Manchester, where Adolphe became chairman of the chemists and distillers merchants Sparks, White, and Company Limited, based in Deansgate in Manchester, which produced perfume fragrances and fine oils. When they first came to Manchester they lived at Clarence Lodge in Victoria Park, before they moved to a house called 'Saville' on Lower Park Road in Victoria Park (now known as Ward Hall). His younger brother, Eric (born in 1869) worked at the same company as a chemist's clerk and lived with them. Also at the address was his nephew, Fred Hans Saville (born at Charlottenberg in Berlin in 1896).

Adolphe also had a sister named Marianne, who married an N N Goldstein. They had a daughter named Rosa 'Rose', who was born in Poland in 1888, and became Mrs Paul Josef Danby (born with the surname Dambitsch, in Berlin in 1886).

Adolphe had the good business sense to diversify into the perfumery trade, which was booming in England, and he hoped to take advantage of the expanding market in America, so he planned a trip to the States. He selected a collection of fragrances, which he put into sixty-five small glass bottles. They seem to be the fragrances that were popular in the Edwardian period such as Lily of the Valley, Blushing Rose and Orange Blossom.

He boarded *Titanic* at Southampton as a first-class passenger, which cost him £30. He carried his precious bottles in a black leather satchel bearing the name 'Adolfe Saalfeld and Co'. His cabin was number 106 on C Deck, opposite the cabin of John Jacob Astor VI, the wealthiest man on board.

Paul Danby travelled to Southampton with his uncle-in-law, and together they had a look around the ship on the day that Adolphe boarded. Paul wrote a letter in German to his wife back in Manchester, giving Adolphe's accommodation a glowing report. Adolph wrote to his wife stating that he too was very impressed by the ship. The letter he sent to his wife was probably the very first written on the ship by an early-boarding passenger.

Adolphe was traumatised by his experiences in the sinking and returned to England with his dreams shattered. He was haunted by the horrors and disappointment of *Titanic* tragedy for the rest of his life. He found great difficulty sleeping and would often ask his chauffeur to drive him around the area at night. He died on 5 June 1926, at Kew in Surrey, and he was buried in the Golders Green Cemetery, west London. He was still chairman of his firm, which continued to trade until 1954. *Titanic* tragedy had robbed him of the sweet smell of success, however, when his estate was settled his assets were reportedly worth nearly £47,000.

Paul Danby's association with Germany meant that he was interned for the duration of the Great War, possibly for his own safety, and having become a naturalised British citizen in 1896, it seems that Adolphe and Gertrude adopted his wife Rose to prevent something similar happening to her. On his release, Paul relocated to Amsterdam and ran a successful chemist business. However, when the Germans invaded Holland in 1940 they were among the Jews targeted by the Nazis and he and his wife, and her mother Clara, were arrested and interned in the Sobibor death camp in Poland. Clara was murdered on 2 July 1943, and Paul and Rose were murdered together two weeks later. Their daughter Marguerite 'Margaret' had become a general practitioner in Oss in Holland and used her position to obstruct the Nazi deportation programme by declaring people too sick to travel. Margaret and her sister Ellen survived the war and eventually settled in Canada.

Ellen became a successful ice-skater, who coached her daughter Petra to gain a bronze medal for Canada in the figure skating event at the 1964 Olympic Games, becoming World Champion in the following year. Ellen was inducted into Canada's Sports Hall of Fame in 1996. Margaret died in 1990, aged seventy-nine, and Ellen died in 2016, aged ninety-five.

In 2000 the Submersible vessel *MIR 1* found Adolphe's black leather satchel lying on the seabed and sixty-two of his perfume bottles were salvaged. They spent some time in an unmarked warehouse in Atlanta with thousands of other *Titanic* relics. Pieces of the leather case have been restored, and the case, along with some of the bottles, formed part of the 'Titanic Exhibition' which toured Britain in 2003. One of them was opened to reveal a powerful scent of rose and violet, and visitors to the International Science Festival held in Edinburgh in 2004 were among the first to smell the fragrances for nearly a century, and the 'still-pungent, flowery perfumes' have been recreated for the modern 'retro' market as 'Legacy 2012'.

Adolphe apparently had the Cafe Parisien menu framed and put on display at his Manchester office, and it was given away to an accountant when the office closed down in the mid-1950s. It was sold at a Christie's auction in 1999. The letter he wrote to Gertrude from *Titanic* was sold at a Spinks auction in New York in 2009, while Paul Danby's letter to his wife was sold at auction in 2016.

Joseph George Scarrott

Joe Scarrott was born in Plymouth on 25 April 1878. He was the son of a seaman in the Royal Navy named Joseph Timothy Steven Scarrott (born in Portsea in 1847), and his wife, Bessie Grace Ryder (formerly Truscott, born in Plymouth in 1854, died in 1935). They had married in Plymouth in 1876. Joe had a sister named Elizabeth Bessie, who was born at Portsea in 1882 but she died when she was just one day old, and a brother named Edwin, who was born in Portsea in 1888.

At the time of the 1881 census the family were living at 81 Duke Street in Portsea, Hampshire, and a decade later he and his father were recorded as visitors at 34 East Street in Portsmouth.

His father died in 1897, and on 12 August 1898 Joe married Annie Elizabeth Till, who had been born in Portsmouth in 1879. A son named George Joseph was born in 1899, but he died in 1903.

However, on 15 September 1907, Joe married a second woman named Agnes Laura Payne, who lived not far away from his home.

He worked as an able seaman on various White Star vessels during his career, and other ships of the line, and he transferred from the *Kildonan Castle* to *Titanic*, giving his address as 36 Albert Road in Southampton, where he was living with his sister, Elizabeth.

On returning to Hampshire after the sinking, Joe continued his career at sea. However, in February 1914 he was tried for bigamy. He stated that his marriage to Annie had been an unhappy one and they were separated several times, and on wanting to make a family home he married Agnes instead. His relationship with Agnes had been a happy one until he confessed to his bigamous act during a fit of depression and Agnes reported him to the authorities. 'The accused was given very good character, and the Judge sentenced him to only a month's imprisonment.'

He was widowed in 1915, and married again in Middlesex in 1919, to Elizabeth Minnie Henrietta Koster (born in 1888 at Tower Hamlets in Middlesex, died in 1981 at Southend-on-Sea).

Joe died in Rochford in Essex, on 19 August 1938, aged sixty, and he was buried in an unmarked grave at Sutton Road Cemetery in Southend.

Jonathan Shepherd

Jonathan Shepherd was born on 31 March 1880, in Whitehaven. He was one of nine children of James Bromley Shepherd (born at Whitehaven in 1850), who was an architect and surveyor, and Johanna Elizabeth (formerly Glover, born in 1851 at Abbeyfeale in Limerick, Ireland). They had married at Great Sankey near Warrington, on Christmas Day, 25 December 1866. One of nine children, Jonathan's known siblings were: Joseph Arthur (born in 1873); Frances (born in the United States in 1874); Ruth Dixon (born in Whitehaven, and christened at St James's, Whitehaven, on 14 February 1875); Margaret Honora (born in Whitehaven about 3 September 1876); Joseph (born in 1885) and Harold (born in 1889).

At the time of the disaster, a newspaper reported:

> Some forty years ago the father himself had a miraculous escape from being lost at sea. At that time he was in America and had booked his passage on the City of Boston which left New York for England, and was never heard of again. She foundered in the Atlantic. Providentially, Mr Shepherd changed his plans at the last minute, and did not sail on the vessel. His family were not aware of the true circumstance, and they mourned him as dead for six months.

The 1881 census records the family living at 12 Lowther Street, Whitehaven, and a decade later they lived at 9 Church Street. They eventually moved to Blackburn, where the 1901 census records them living at 4 Caton Terrace, although James is recorded as living at a different address in Accrington, where he worked as a textile machine fitter. By 1911 the family are recorded as living at 27 London Road.

Jonathan served an apprenticeship with the firm of boilermakers named James Davenport of the Canal Foundry in Blackburn, after which he secured a place as second engineer on a steamer that traded with China and Japan, and he was in those waters during the war in the Far East in 1894–95. It was noted at the time 'The presents he brought home included a beautiful tea service, a valuable pair of Satsuma vases, and choice Japanese pictures'. He worked for Howard and Bullough, a textile machine manufacturers based at the Globe Works in Accrington, and Hadfields Steelworks of Sheffield, before moving to Liverpool to commence a seagoing career with the W S Kennaugh and Sons shipping company of Liverpool. Jonathan also served on ships owned by James Chambers and Company as part of the Lancashire Shipping Company based in Liverpool. He joined the White Star Line after obtaining his first-class marine engineer's certificate at Liverpool in 1907.

He served first on the *Adriatic* and then on the *Olympic* when the collision occurred with HMS *Hawke*. On that occasion he showed remarkable presence of mind, for as soon as he heard the crash he realised that something serious had happened, and at once closed the watertight doors. As he did so he was up to his knees in water.

Chief Engineer Joseph Bell, a fellow native of Cumberland, selected Jonathan to accompany him on *Titanic*. However, his father stated:

> My lad did not want to go on *Titanic*. He would rather have stopped on the *Olympic*. But, Mr Bell, when he was promoted to larger vessels belonging to the White Star Company chose my son to go with him every time. It was an honour that we appreciated, but somehow or another in this instance my boy was reluctant to change ships. Still, he felt it to be his duty, and he went.

His place of residence when he signed on *Titanic* as a junior assistant engineer was as a lodger at 16 Bellevue Terrace in Nicholstown, Southampton.

Having visited his home in Blackburn a few weeks before going to Belfast, the local paper reported that at the time:

> He was not so jolly when he went away, as he seemed to have an idea that something would happen.
>
> Mr Shepherd has another son at sea, Joseph, who is with the Bibby Line, and is now on his way home from Rangoon. He (Jonathan) was on duty on the evening of 14 April 1912. After the collision he helped the other engineers rig pumps in boiler room Number 5, but broke his leg when he slipped into a raised access plate. Leading fireman Frederick Barrett and engineer Herbert Harvey helped him to the pump-room. Shortly afterwards the nearby bulkheads was breached and Jonathan was left helpless as the waters rose around him.

He was described as 'A fine young fellow. Muscular, and stood six foot without his boots.' His father stated 'My lad would remain on duty, sink or swim. He would stick to his post to the last'.

Christopher Arthur John Shulver (John Dilley)

Christopher Shulver was born at Hackney in east London, on 6 June 1883, and he was baptised at Hackney Wick on 20 June a few weeks later, when his address was given as 1 Salem Place in Waterdene, Homerton, east London. He was the third surviving son in a family of eight surviving children, born between 1877 and 1901, of a stoker named Christopher William Shulver (born at Ipswich in 1851), and Harriett Louisa (formerly Armitage, born at Hackney on 6 April 1859). They had married in London on 15 October 1876. In 1891 they lived at 4 Shepherd's Lane in Hackney, and a decade later they had moved to 8 Link Street in Hackney.

Christopher joined the armed forces in 1902, but little is known of his service or his life at that time except that his father died in 1903. He eventually became involved in petty criminality. He went to jail three times in 1909, twice for stealing and again for criminal damage, and in 1910 he continued stealing, and also received a jail sentence for larceny and receiving stolen goods.

He was living at 44 Threefield Lane in Southampton, and was using the name John Dilley when he signed on *Titanic* on 6 April 1912, stating that he had previously worked on the *Olympic*. He eventually returned to Britain on the *Lapland*, and although he left a good account of what he witnessed he was never asked to give evidence in an official capacity, even though he actually attended the British enquiry. This may have been because of what he knew concerning the fire in the coal bunkers, which the authorities wanted to keep a secret for insurance claim reasons.

On his return to Britain he became involved in a case of fraud when a woman named Annie Sergeant put in a claim to *Titanic* Relief Fund by stating she was married to John Dilley, and the committee awarded her £1. She was found out as a fraudulent claimer when she tried to get more money using a different name. She claimed to be Christopher's sweetheart, to which he replied 'She is everybody's sweetheart!'. Being exposed as a woman of ill repute with no fixed abode, she was sent to jail.

His mother remarried in 1913 and lived with her new husband and several of Christopher's siblings at 50 Chalgrove Road in Hackney. However, Chris continued to fall foul of the law, being convicted and jailed for stealing on three occasions in 1913 and 1914.

When the Great War broke out he was still in prison, but on his release he travelled to Shoreditch to sign up as an engineer with the Royal Field Artillery, giving his address as 19 Chalgrove Road in Hackney, and his next-of-kin as his mother. He was described as being just under 5ft 5in tall, weighing 148lb, with brown hair and blue eyes, and he had a tattoo of a ship on his left forearm. It was thought that he never married, but the electoral register in 1919 for 19 Chalgrove Road includes an unidentified woman named Caroline Shulver.

He served mainly as a driver, and even in the service of his country he had a chequered career. He was confined to barracks on many occasions for various offences such as being absent from parades and speaking improperly to his superiors. He was sent to France in February 1916, and his brother Joseph was killed in action in France on 13 March 1916. In October 1917 he received a shrapnel wound in his shoulder when a shell exploded near him. He was invalided home to the UK and was demobbed in March 1920. For his service he received 'Pip, Squeak and Wilfred' the affectionate names given to the three campaign medals given for service in the Great War – the 1914-15 Star; the British War Medal, 1914-18; and the Allied Victory Medal.

After the war he went back to work for the White Star Line, and used the name John Arthur Dilley. He is said to have walked all the way from Cardiff to Liverpool to find work, and for his effort he gained employment as a fireman on the RMS *Adriatic*. On 11 August 1922, he was one of several men who were working in one of the coal bunkers when an accidental explosion killed and injured many of them, and Chris was one of the fatalities. He died from burns and shock.

Newspaper reports at the time stated:

> Two firemen, Stephen McGuinness and A J Dilley were sleeping on number 3 hatch. McGuinness's body was blown overboard. By a strange freak of the explosion, Dilley, wrapped in a blanket, was shot with a straw mattress up to the starboard side of the promenade deck, under the bridge, where he was found still lying on the mattress with his cheek still resting on the right hand, just as if he had been slumbering when death overtook him. Dilley had walked from Cardiff to Liverpool to get a job in the ship.
>
> Today while the sun was sinking two victims were enshrouded in the Union Jack and sent to rest in the deep while 1500 people on board stood at reverent silence.

He was buried at sea at Latitude 41 25 N – Longitude 51 41 W.

His mother had suffered the loss of most of her children at very young ages, and she had been made a widow for a second time when she died in Hackney in 1938.

Sarah Agnes Stap

Sarah Agnes Stap was born at sea on board her father's ship HMS *Mystery* in the Bay of Bengal, on 1 August 1864, and she was baptised in London in the following year. She was the second oldest daughter in the family of five children born between 1862 and 1875 to a master mariner named Henry Stap, who was born at Skipsea near Bridlington in the East Riding of Yorkshire on 11 February 1829, and his wife, Stella (formerly Cawkwell, born at Bermondsey in south London on 14 October 1835). Her parents had married at Mile End in London on 31 August 1861. Henry Stap held several commands in the White Star and Leyland Lines. One of her younger brothers, Henry, became a teacher, and he was master at the Oake's Institute Grammar School in Liverpool for twenty-five years until his death in 1933.

The 1871 census records the family living at Willesly Road in Wanstead, Essex, and a decade later they had moved to 3 St Phillips' Terrace in Kensington, London. For the 1891 and 1901 censuses they were recorded as living at 48 Church Street in Seacombe, Wallasey.

It would seem that Sarah had already decided to follow in her father's footsteps and go to sea, because she was not listed on the 1901 census. Her mother died in 1903, and she was buried in Rake Lane Cemetery in Wallasey. Her father and several of her siblings were residing at 41 Bidstan Avenue in Cloughton, Birkenhead, at the time of the 1911 census.

Sarah later stated that at the time of the disaster she had been at sea for about twelve years:

> I was on board the *Olympic* when she collided with the *Hawke*. I was on board the *Baltic* when she made her maiden voyage (29 June 1904), and also on board the *Adriatic* when she made her first trip (8 May 1907). My father, Captain Stap, was in the employ of the White Star Company, but has now retired.

She arrived back in Birkenhead on 2 May 1912, and two days later she told the local newspaper of her experiences. Her father died in 1914.

The entire family were eventually buried in Rake Lane Cemetery. The original memorial at the grave bore the single word 'Stap', until a new commemorative headstone was placed next to it in 2014.

Leonard Taylor

Len Taylor was born at Glossop in Derbyshire on 1 April 1893. He was the second of two sons in the family of five children of a baths attendant named Frederick John Taylor (born in Glossop in 1866), and his wife Alice (formerly Rostron, born in Bolton in 1860); who had married on 26 November 1890, and made their home at 5 Cliff Road in Glossop. At the time of his birth the family home was at 108 Charlestown, and Len was baptised in the Whitfield district of the town on 21 May 1893.

In about 1897 they moved to live at 7 Boothroyd Street in Blackpool, where Fred Taylor eventually took up employment as head masseur at the Imperial Hydropathic Hotel, which was opened at St Anne's-on-Sea in 1910 (later named the Majestic). A decade later the family home was at 6 Sherbourne Road, North Shore, Blackpool. Len was educated at Claremont School, where he became a champion swimmer, and on leaving he took up employment as a baths attendant (probably at the well-known Derby Baths).

Len spotted an advertisement for *Titanic* staff and he was 'over the moon' when he gained a position on 6 April 1912, as a junior attendant and masseur in the ship's Turkish bath, for a salary of £4 a month. His seniors were J Bertram Crosbie, and Walter Ennis of Southport, and there were two women named Annie Caton and Maud Slocombe. At the age of nineteen he was the youngest member of staff.

The three Turkish bath men were all lost in the disaster, but the two women were saved, and if the body of Len Taylor was recovered it was never identified.

Len's sister Florence is said to have talked 'proudly and emotionally' about him. She used to have meetings with other people associated with the disaster and it was her belief that the ship would have stayed afloat even after it hit the iceberg, and that it was an explosion of gas that caused the vessel to split in half and sealed its fate.

When she passed away her family came upon a case full of letters, which included the one he wrote to his parents from Queenstown. The letter was auctioned and ended up in the United States, and it was auctioned again in 2012 and was bought by a collector in Boston, Massachusetts.

Thomas Threlfall

Tom Threlfall was born on 19 October 1867, in Liverpool, and he was baptised at St Peter's Church on 10 November that year. Most of the places associated with Tom's life seem to be situated in the Vauxhall-Everton districts on either side of Scotland Road. He was the only son and the oldest of six children born between 1867 and 1894 to a carter named James Threlfall (born in 1844), and his wife, Grace (formerly Wharton, born in 1843). Both parents were natives of Liverpool, and they had married in 1866. At that time of Tom's birth the family were living in Hornby Street in Liverpool. In 1881 they lived in Portland Street. The 1891 census has them living at 68 China Street in Everton, and Tom had gone to sea, working as a trimmer on *Tauric*.

On 17 May 1892 he married Margaret Downes, who was born in Liverpool on 31 May 1870, the daughter of Simon Downes and Margaret (formerly Meara). Their first child, Margaret, was born on 22 June 1894.

After his marriage, he worked on several ships and seemed to change addresses quite a lot. By February 1903 he was working as a fireman aboard *Cedric*, and gave his address as 85 Ellison Street in Liverpool. He was working aboard the *Baltic* until 1906, when he began working as a greaser aboard *Empress of Britain*, and in the following year he became leading fireman on the *Majestic*. During this time his address was given as Ashfield Street.

A daughter named Nora was born in 1909, and the 1911 census records that Tom was absent at sea, probably on *Olympic*, while his family lived with his wife's mother, at 128 St Martin's Court in Liverpool. He joined *Titanic* on 6 April 1912 as a leading fireman. Tom gave an account of his experience during the sinking until he was rescued in lifeboat 14.

In 1913 he was appointed to the charge of the Liverpool branch of the recently established British Seafarers' Union based in South John Street. During the First World War he served aboard the SS *Arcadian*, which was responsible for transporting wounded soldiers from Salonika in Greece to Alexandria in Egypt. On 15 April 1917, five years to the day after Titanic disaster, his ship was hit by a German torpedo and sank in about five minutes. Tom survived and later stated 'It was the same day of the week and the same date of the month that *Titanic* went down … and I have come safely out of both affairs'. When asked which of the two experiences did he think was the worst, he replied 'Well, Titanic stopped afloat for a couple of hours and we had time to turn around, but of course you could not live in the water that night. This time we had calm sea and warm weather, and you had a chance, but with *Titanic* you died in the water almost as soon as you got in.'

Tom's wife died in 1929, and he died in Liverpool on 10 January 1934, aged sixty-six.

Samuel Francis Webb

Sam Webb was born in Salford, on 24 November 1883, the son of Frederick Charles Webb (born in 1860), a chair maker, and his wife Elizabeth (formerly Raby, born in 1864). They were originally from Bristol, and Fred and Elizabeth had married in Manchester around the time of Sam's birth.

Sam was apparently raised in Bristol and the surrounding area by his grandparents, Samuel Webb (born in 1838, died in 1909), also a chair maker, and his wife, Susan (formerly Roberts born in 1837, died in 1902). He was listed with them on the 1891 and 1901 censuses at 2 Clift Place, Weston in Gordano, Somerset. On the latter record he was described as a printer. Following the death of his grandparents and by the time of the 1911 census Sam was listed as living with an uncle and aunt, William and Mary Ann Burnell, at 27 Lancaster Street in Bristol, and he was described as an unmarried colliery hewer. He seemingly went to sea shortly after and worked on the *Olympic*.

When he signed on *Titanic*, on 6 April 1912, he gave his local address as the Sailors' Home, (Southampton) and his previous ship as the *Olympic*. As a trimmer he could expect to earn monthly wages of £5 10s. Sam Webb died in the sinking. His body, if recovered, was never identified.

Thomas Arthur Whiteley

Tom Whiteley was born on 3 April 1894, at 29 Queen's Road (now Queenston Road) in the Albert Park district of West Didsbury, Manchester, the only son of Arthur Whiteley and his wife, Elizabeth (formerly Ross, born in Edinburgh in about 1864). Elizabeth was already widowed with a daughter named Isabella, and had been living with her family at a hotel in Leeds, when she married Arthur in 1892. Tom's sister, Violet Stuart, was born in 1897, and in 1901 they lived at Cross Lane in Marple, Cheshire. By 1911 Tom's father had died, and they were living in London, where Elizabeth and Isabella became involved in West End theatre work. It is believed that Tom travelled a lot in his early days and in 1911 he was said to be in Italy. He had served on the *Olympic*, and when he signed on *Titanic* he gave his address as 29 St John's Park in Highgate, north London.

On being rescued by *Carpathia*, Tom was taken to St Vincent's Hospital in New York with a fractured right leg and numerous bruises. Soon after leaving hospital he appeared at the Merrimack Square Theatre for a week to give talks and answer questions about his experiences. He filed a law suit against the White Star Line in which he claimed negligent steering and that *Titanic* had been unseaworthy. The case was scheduled for March 1914 but it never came to court. He served as a driver with 41 Wing, Royal Flying Corps during the Great War, and is believed to have been injured in the face or throat around this time. The next reference is to a steward named as 'Thos Whitely', who worked on the *Celtic* during a voyage from Liverpool to New York in 1924 and later deserted.

The name Tom Whitely and other variations of his surname begin to appear in press publicity and playbills for some notable Broadway stage shows in 1925. In 1927 he moved to Hollywood, making comedies with Lupino Lane. In 1929 he played the sergeant major in the film version of *Journey's End*, which premiered at the London Savoy, about life in the trenches during the Great War, which was a great success. From 1931 to 1933 he played small parts in MGM films, then he went to Puerto Rico during Christmas 1935 to make plans for the making of a film about the sinking of the *Lusitania*, but the projected movie never materialised.

During the Second World War, Tom was a warrant officer with 87 Squadron, Royal Air Force, and served during the North Africa landings in 1942. As the invasion force progressed up the Adriatic coast, WO Whiteley went with them. However, on 11 October 1944, in circumstances that remain a mystery, Tom died on his way to a hospital in Fano, apparently as the result of cardiac problems, aged fifty. He lies buried at the Ancona War Cemetery in Italy.

Elizabeth Anne Wilkinson

Lizzie Wilkinson was born on 3 February 1882, at 42 Hadfield Street in Newton Heath, Manchester, being baptised at St Ann's Church on 15 March. Another source says St Andrews Church on 13 November 1884. She was the daughter of William H Wilkinson (born 1855), a wheelwright, a craftsman who repairs wooden wheels, who was a native of Rochdale, and his wife, Mary Anne (formerly Jordan, born in 1847), who was a native of Bradford. They had married at St Barnabas' Church in Miles Platting, Manchester, on 30 December 1877. Elizabeth had an older brother named William (born in 1880).

At the time of the 1891 census they were living at 14 Mount Street in Swinton, Salford, where her father had become a paper dealer. A decade later they had moved to 2 Clarendon Road in Swinton. They are also believed to have lived in Moorfield House in Pendlebury. On 20 May 1907, in Salford, she married a twenty-four-year-old butcher named Samuel Wilkinson, who had been born in Denton in Manchester on 4 July 1882. His father was a paper dealer and came from Rochdale, and it is a possibility that Lizzie and Sam were second cousins. At the time of the 1911 census they lived at 47 Oldham Road in Failsworth, north Manchester.

Lizzie boarded *Titanic* on a joint ticket as a second-class passenger, and she was described as the new wife of Harry Bertram Faunthorpe, a businessman, travelling to Philadelphia. They told others on the ship that they planned to honeymoon in California.

Under the heading 'Failsworth Woman Saved' an Oldham newspaper reported soon after the disaster 'Elizabeth Ann Wilkinson, wife of Samuel Wilkinson, of 47 Oldham Road, Failsworth, was a second cabin passenger on Titanic. She has telegraphed from New York: 'Am safe – Lizzie'.

Lizzie escaped in lifeboat 16, but Harry drowned. According to the Red Cross, his body was recovered at sea and more than $1,000 worth of jewellery was taken from his clothing. The body was forwarded to Mrs Faunthorpe, care of William Springfield in Philadelphia, where he was buried. Lizzie went to stay with her cousin, John Devine, at 669 Brooklyn Street, Philadelphia, later staying at her uncle's home, where she was reported as being ill from the strain of the experience. She sued the White Star Company for $10,000 in the Federal Court, for the loss of who she stated was her 'husband'.

All the publicity meant that her deceit had been exposed, but nevertheless, Sam accepted her back into his life. However, there is speculation that they eventually divorced and both remarried.

James William Cheetham Witter

James Witter was born on 23 June 1880, and the 1881 census has the family living at Holly House Green in Aughton near Ormskirk. He was the second son in the family of five children born between 1865 and 1877 to an agricultural labourer named James Witter (born at Halsall near Ormskirk in 1840), and his wife, Ann (formerly Dutton, born at Halsall in 1841). They had married in 1867. Their grandfather, James, married Elizabeth Cheetham, in Maghull, on 15 June 1840, hence James' unusual third Christian name.

A decade later the family were living at 14 Parkinson Road in Walton near Ormskirk.

By 1908 he was living in the Southampton area, where he married at Woolston near Southampton on 10 April 1908, his new wife being Hannah (born at Selkirk on 29 May 1881), the daughter of a wool weaver named Edward Greaves and his wife Hannah. The 1911 census gives their home as 56 Porchester Road in Woolston, although James is not listed.

Ernest Archer was a close neighbour, and he later became a survivor of *Titanic* disaster.

Jim and Hannah had four children who took the surname Cheetham-Witter. Richard S was born at South Stoneham near Southampton in 1908, but he lived for only a day; James Richard (born on 21 August 1911 at Woolston); Elizabeth 'Betty' (born in 1914) and Jack (born in 1917).

Jim transferred from *Olympic*, and signed on to *Titanic* on 4 April 1912 as a second-class smoke room steward.

Jim signed on to *Oceanic* on 10 July 1912, and remained at sea for many more years with the White Star Line and then with Cunard White Star, serving on many of the great transatlantic liners, including *Queen Mary* and *Queen Elizabeth*. He assisted Walter Lord when he wrote the book *A Night to Remember*, but he rarely spoke of the disaster, which was said to have haunted him for the rest of his life.

James Witter died in Southampton on 12 September 1956, at the age of eighty, and he was buried in an unmarked grave at the South Stoneham Cemetery in Southampton.

William Wynn

William Wynn was born in Chester, on 13 November 1870. Most of what is known about him comes from an article that appeared in the *Chester Observer* on 14 January 1939, under the title: A TITANIC DISASTER SURVIVOR: Chester Man's 55 Adventurous Years at Sea. The article was published by a local reporter (J F), who was a passenger on the *Stirling Castle* of the Union Star Line when he interviewed Bill.

The article stated: 'As a boy he attended Holy Trinity Boys' School (in Vicarage Road, Hoole). Soon after his eleventh birthday he became an errand boy at Bollands (Tea and Coffee Merchants on Eastgate Row), and then at a tailor's shop in Foregate Street; later he acted as a conductor on the trams. But he always felt the "call of the sea" as he termed it. About this time he was mixing with a number of young lads, among whom were some who might have led him into trouble; he was glad therefore when an old lady interested herself on his behalf, and she was instrumental in getting him posted to the training ship *Clio*, moored off Bangor in North Wales, which had its main offices at 29 Eastgate Row, not far from Bollands. He stated that he was known as 'Punch' Wynn as a lad in Chester.

There are no census records for him, but the report states that 'He lost track of his relatives – never heard of one since he lost his father in 1890'.

Merchant Navy records later in his fifty-five-year career state that he was '5 feet 5 inches tall, with grey eyes and hair, and a fresh complexion. His distinguishing marks included a tattoo of "faith, hope and charity" on his right arm, and clasped hands on his left arm.'

The report continued: 'When he was 16 he was sent to Liverpool, where he shipped in a 100 ton schooner. But he did not get enough to eat and sought and obtained a job in a bigger vessel. In 1888, while he was employed on a large sailing ship, The *Garfield*, he nearly lost his life in a typhoon while on a voyage from India to New York. In February 1898 he was employed by an American Line, and on 6 February 1898, he was aboard the USS *St Louis* as an able seaman when that ship mounted a rescue of passengers and crew from SS *Veendam* of the Holland-American Line when she collided with a sunken wreck and foundered. When the Spanish-American war broke out on 21 April 1898, he joined the American navy 'For the Duration' – (until 13 August 1898). The South African War broke out (1899), and he was soon employed in ships sailing to and from South Africa with troops and invalids.

'The war over (1902), he joined the White Star Line, where he was on the quartermaster's staff of the *Oceanic*.'

In late 1907 in Southampton, he married Eliza Kate (formerly Abbott, born in 1880 at Lockerley in Hampshire). In 1911 the family home was at 77 Church Street in Shirley, Southampton.

The article added: 'One day the men were assembled, and he was chosen to proceed to Belfast, where he found he was posted to *Titanic*' (on 25 March 1912). He signed on as W Wynn, and most official documentation confirms that his first name was William, although his inquiry testimony was given as Walter Wynn. He gave his address as 81 Church Street.

'In 1914 he was afloat in the Olympic when war was declared, and he 'carried on' during the period of the Great War in different ships, finishing up in the Persian Gulf. He could tell some stories about this period of his life.'

His wife, Eliza, died on 24 June 1930, aged fifty, while they were still living at 81 Church Street in Shirley. They had no children.

In 1939 he was serving aboard the *Stirling Castle*, when the report stated 'Punch Wynn is still going strong. He has never had a day's illness since he went to sea, and he has been over 55 years a seaman. He is indeed a fine example of merchant sailor, and a credit to "Ye Ancient Citye".'

Bill died in 1945, at the age of seventy-five. He was buried in an unmarked grave at Hollybrook Cemetery in Southampton.

Appendix

The following article appeared in several newspapers three days after the disaster. It touches on the contradictory reports given out by the Americans, and points out some of the issues of the time.

TITANIC CATASTROPHE
HOW THE NEWS CAME
A STUDY IN CONTRADICTIONS

From our Special Correspondent in London. April 19
One striking feature of the terrible *Titanic* catastrophe was the utterly confusing and contradictory nature of the news cabled from America during the first twenty-four hours after the original intimation that the leviathan liner had collided with an iceberg. This came to hand on Monday evening via Montreal and New York, in the shape of a wireless message from the liner *Virginian*, which reported that she had picked up a message from the *Titanic* announcing the collision and requesting assistance, and that she was hastening to the rescue.

A little later Cape Race reported that the wireless operator on the *Titanic* reported weather calm and clear, and New York reported that a number of vessels were hastening to the liner's assistance, whilst still later Cape Race reported that the *Titanic* was sinking by the head, and that the women were taken off by the lifeboats.

New York next reported that most of the passengers had been put into the lifeboats, that the sea was calm, and that the White Star line officials in New York stated that the *Virginian* was standing by, so that there was no danger of loss of life.

Then the Exchange Telegraph Company sent out a message from Halifax stating that all the passengers were taken off *Titanic* at 3.30 a.m. (10.30 English time), and Halifax sent per Montreal a report that the *Titanic* was still afloat and making her way slowly to Halifax with her forward compartments full of water, but was expected to make port.

Next New York reported through from the *Virginian* that the *Titanic* was sinking, and Boston came along with a message from St John's, Newfoundland, to the effect that the stricken liner was struggling slowly towards Cape Race. Later still Reuters from New York reported that *Titanic* had sunk at 2.20 a.m. (Monday), and that no lives were lost, but quickly followed this up with a White Star official statement that 'probably a number of lives had been lost', but that no definite estimate could be made until 'it was known positively whether the *Parisian* and the *Virginian* had any rescued passengers on board'.

Within five minutes of despatching this wire the Reuter's New York man cabled an official statement from the White Star Company to the effect that Captain Haddock, of the *Olympic*, had sent a wireless that the *Titanic* sank at 2.20 am on Monday, later all the passengers and crew had been lowered into lifeboats and transferred to the *Virginian*, and that the steamer *Carpathia*, with several hundred passengers from the *Titanic*, were on the way to New York.

At 8.40 pm Reuter's reported from New York an admission by the White Star officials that many lives had been lost, and Cape Race simultaneously reported a wireless message from the *Olympic* stating that the steamer *Carpathia* reached *Titanic*'s position at daybreak, but found boats and wreckage only. She reported that the *Titanic* foundered about 2.20 am in latitude 41 degrees, 16 min, longitude. 50 degrees, 14 min. All the *Titanic's* boats are accounted for. About 675 souls have been saved of the crew and passengers. The latter are nearly all women and children.

The Leyland liner *California* is remaining and searching the vicinity of the disaster. The *Carpathia* is 'returning to New York with the survivors'.

Imaginative Messages

At 9 p.m. the *Times*, own correspondent intervened with the following: 'The International Mercantile Marine Company has received a private message from the *Olympic* that the *Titanic* foundered at 2.20 this morning, and that the *Carpathia* is proceeding to New York with passengers. Vice-President Franklin positively refused to give out the full text of a private message, which leads to the belief that possibly there has been loss of life. Later Mr Franklin said that he could not state with certainty that everybody had been saved. Half an hour later Reuters reported that Mr. Franklin admitted that there had been 'horrible loss of life', and stated that he had no information to disprove a press dispatch from Cape Race, which stated that only 675 passengers and crew had been rescued. A quarter-of-an-hour afterwards Reuters sent the evil tidings that the White Star people frankly admitted that probably only 675 out of the *Titanic* passengers had been saved. Even later messages were to a great measure conflicting, and it was not until late on Tuesday evening that we were in receipt of what we could accept as really authentic news concerning the disaster.

From what has now transpired it would appear that many of the earlier messages received from America must have been either purely imaginative efforts, or that the wireless messages received at the Cape Race station and elsewhere from the various liners hastening to the rescue of *Titanic* got terribly mutilated or mixed up with one another. The air within a few hundred miles of Cape Race would seem to have been alive with wireless messages from a dozen liners, all seeking to obtain or impart information. To make matters worse, it appears that a number of amateurs possessing private wireless installations were taking advantage of the occasion to test their apparatus, with the result that serious interruptions to official messages were caused. Whether these things in any way added to the disaster cannot yet be stated, but it is clear that in certain cases it might have such a result, and the question arises whether the time is not ripe for an international convention regulating the sending of wireless messages.

Lies, Lies, and American News

The false news sent from America was by no means confined to the first day of the disaster. During Wednesday and Thursday all sorts of utterly unreliable matter were poured through the cables. Much of it has proved so wide of the fact as to suggest that it was deliberately invented to serve some special purpose. One message received from New York gave what purported to be a description of the foundering of *Titanic* as received by wireless from the steamer *Bruce*. It is now absolutely certain that the *Bruce* was never even in touch with *Titanic*, or with any steamer near the scene of the disaster, and that no one on board of *Bruce* sent any wireless message to anyone anywhere concerning the catastrophe. By the time the faked story came to hand English people had well-nigh emptied their self of its credibility, deep though it is, and had settled down to wait with what calmness could muster for the true story which they knew must come before the week was out. It came to hand in the shape of a statement said to have been issued to the Press by 'a committee of survivors' and began: 'We, the undersigned …' But strange to say, the signatories' names were not appended to the statement it received in England. They are reported to have made the statement 'in order to forestall any sensational and exaggerated reports'. but curiously enough, though their report is the briefest of those to hand, it contains more sensational matter to the inch than any! Here are some of the contents of this unknown committee's precious report of 'facts' which have come to our knowledge, and which I believe to be true:

> On Sunday, April 14, 1912, at about 11.40 on a cold starlit night, the ship struck an iceberg.
> Rockets were fired at intervals.
> Captain Smith shot himself on the bridge.
> The chief engineer likewise committed suicide.
> Three Italians were shot to death in the struggle for the lifeboats.

The passengers who were first told of the captain's end said that two attempts were necessary before he was successful in ending his life. His brother officers wrested the revolver from his hand in the library, but he broke away to the bridge and shot himself through the mouth.

All is not yet clear, but this one thing is certain. There was no panic on board, not a mad rush for the lifeboats, and no shooting of men, Italian or otherwise, and so far as other survivors stories can he relied upon Captain Smith when last seen by eyewitnesses was at his post on the bridge.

The underwriters of Lloyds by the way are not very sure over the quality of *Titanic* intelligence supplied by the Americans. The market was first shocked by the Lloyd's first telegram from Cape Race, giving the wireless messages from *Titanic*, and a rate of 50 per cent was at once quoted for reinsurance which subsequently advanced to 60 per cent. That is to say some underwriters, who were not heavily committed, or thought they had reason to be optimistic, were ready to assume the original risk at that late. Then came news that the vessel was heading slowly to Halifax, that she was in tow of the *Virginian*, and that all the passengers had been saved. Finally, came Mr. Franklin's statement that the vessel was unsinkable and the rate gradually declined to 50, to 45, to 30, and finally to 25 per cent, or lower. The rate could hardly have fallen in a more striking fashion had the 'news' been inspired with the intention of deluding the market.

According to the old tag, there were three classes of lies – 'Lies, lies, and statistics'. Today one feels inclined to substitute 'American news' for 'statistics'.

Dangerous Luxury

The question of an inadequate provision of lifeboats on the *Titanic* is beginning to be discussed, and the suggestion is made that if there had been enough boats for everybody there would not have been such an appalling death-toll. It is said that the mad competition of the Transatlantic lines to outrival one another in luxurious fittings has caused space to be sacrificed to palatial accommodation which should be occupied by life-saving devices. The comment is made that the race for splendour in ocean travel has received a severe blow, which must cause a reaction in favour of liners carrying more small boats. Many questions have been addressed to the President of the Board of Trade, the department responsible for the legislation of this matter, and from Mr. Buxton's replies in the House of Commons it appears that *Titanic* carried 16 boats for 990 passengers; 4 boats for 188 passengers; total boat accommodation, 1,178 Lifebuoys, 48 lifebelts, 3,560 vessel certified to carry 3,547 souls: actual number on board, 2,208 souls. Mr. Buxton also stated that under existing regulations the boat accommodation is founded on the tonnage of the vessel, and not on the number of its passengers.

A Millionaires' Trip

The *Titanic* was essentially a liner for millionaires, and on the maiden voyage quite a number of very wealthy men took passage by her. The liner herself was valued at £1,750,000, with fittings, the cargo, valuables on board, mails, etc, are estimated of the value of at least £1,000,000. Among the passengers were men representing a minimum of £120,000,000 of capital. They included: Colonel J. J. Astor - £30,000,000; Mr. B. Guggenheim - 20,000,000, Mr. J. Straus - 10,000,000, Mr. G Widener - 10,000,000, Mr. W. Roebling - 5,000,000. Other wealthy men, many of them millionaires, included Mr. J. B. Brady, Mr. Howard Case, Mr. J. B. Cummings, Mr. T. P. Franklin, Mr Hermann Klaher, Mr. D. A.Y. Marvin, Mr. V. Payne, Mr. Frederick Sutton, and Mr. G. A. Vick.

Honeymoon Tragedies

One of the saddest features of the disaster was the number of newly-married people on board, some of them on their honeymoon trip. Doubtless the new vessel had been chosen for the voyage to New York on account of the special facilities for privacy and amusement, coupled with comfort and elegance. Among these couples were Colonel and Mrs. J. J. Astor. They were married in the autumn in the United States, and had spent the winter in Egypt, returning by way of Paris, where they had been entertaining friends. Mrs. Astor is among the saved. Mr. D. A. Y. Marvin, who also was on board with his young wife, was married in January last, and the happy couple came to England, where some of Mrs. Marvin's relatives reside. Mr. Marvin was returning to his business as head of a large cinematograph firm. Mrs. Marvin was saved. One of the branch managers of Messrs. Liptons, who was married in the middle of March, Mr. McNamee, had been appointed on his marriage to a responsible position in New York, and he was taking his bride to the new country. Both are believed to be lost. Mr. Alfred Davies, of West Bromwich, was married on Monday week last. With his two brothers, his brother-in-law, and his bride, he had a suite on deck B. All are believed to be drowned. On Sunday week last a pretty wedding took place at Norwich, and the newly-wedded couple, Mr. and Mrs. Beana, left for Southampton and joined the *Titanic* on their honeymoon trip to America. Both are happily saved. Only a fortnight earlier a young engineer, Mr. A. Sedgwick, of St. Helens, was married. On Wednesday week he left for New York on the *Titanic*, en route to South America, to take up an appointment. It was arranged that his bride should follow later. His name is not on the list of survivors.

'Women First'

The fact that so large a proportion of women were saved from the wreck compared with men is adduced on many sides as an example of the innate chivalry which characterises men in spite of the view held by many women of today, particularly many prominent suffragists claim that chivalry is a thing of the past. A prominent anti-suffragist, who gave his opinion freely, said, 'It seems to me that the behaviour, so far as I've know it, of the passengers on the *Titanic* is a crushing answer to what are called the "demands" of the suffragists, especially the militant kind. Sensible people know that chivalry is not dead, and is never likely to be so long as attraction between the sexes continues. The disaster of the *Titanic* only shows how deep the roots of chivalry are. After all, to treat the matter dispassionately and coldly, who is of the most effective use in the world, the millionaire who owns railroad systems or the Swedish lady's maid? And yet the lady's maid escapes and the millionaire goes down, although his loss to the material world is incalculably greater. But it will be a bail world when the 'equality' of the suffragists prevails and man and woman make a dash for the boats together.'

Mrs. Annie Kenney (one of the organising secretaries of the Women's Social and Political Union) takes a different view. She says 'I have a great admiration for the heroism shown by the men, but it is possible to exalt this heroism on too much a plane of chivalry. In the first place, it is so natural as to be accounted almost a natural view that women and children should be saved first; children because childhood is sacred and women because they are so necessary to the race that they cannot be spared. At a crisis such as this it must be admitted that the lives of the women are more useful to the race than those of the men. If it is insisted that for the men to recognise this view and act upon it is chivalry, and I am not loath to admit it, then I think it is a moment to insist then the everyday chivalry of women which goes on always and usually unrecognised. Women cheerfully starve for their husbands and children. I have lived among the poorer classes and know it, and starving is a much more slow and painful death than drowning. Say man is chivalrous at moments of strife, if you will, but realise at the same time that in the aggregate the balance of chivalry is on the part of the woman.'

Mrs. Cecil Chapman thinks the feeling of the suffragists is that they would have preferred to meet their fate alongside their husbands. Far from the age of chivalry being dead, the women would like to share danger with men, for the women are as chivalrous as men. I think that the men who launched in the House of Commons at the women they put to torture showed that chivalry is very dead among members of Parliament. But there was no lack of chivalry on the part of the men on the *Titanic*.'

Bibliography and Research References

A & E Television Networks, *Titanic: The Complete Story* (TV Documentary), 1994
Aberdeen Press and Journal for 14 August 1922
Ancestry.co.uk
Atlantic Daily Bulletin, The Journal of the British Titanic Society
Ballard, Robert Duane, *The Discovery of Titanic*, 1987
Bancroft, James, *Titanic Struggle: Greater Manchester Victims*, Private, 2019
Beesley, Lawrence, *The Loss of the SS Titanic: Its Story and Its Lessons*, 1912
Belfast Titanic Society
Bell, Chief Engineer Joseph, Letter to his son written on 11 April 1912
Birkenhead News for 4 May 1912 and 3 April 1937
Board of Trade, *The Investigation into the Loss of the* SS *Titanic*, 1912
Boston Globe for 23 April 1912
Bridgwater Mercury for 12 April 1912
British Government, *Loss of the Steamship Titanic: Report of a Formal Investigation into the Circumstances Attending the Foundering on April 15, 1912 of the British Steamship Titanic, of Liverpool, After Striking Ice in or near Latitude 41 - 46 N; Longitude 50 - 14 W, North Atlantic Ocean, as Conducted by the British Government*, 1912
British Titanic Society
Bullock, Stan F, *A Titanic Hero: Thomas Andrews, Shipbuilder*, 1912
Burka, Astra, *My Titanic Uncle (video)*, 2012
Butterworth, John 'Jack', Letter to his girlfriend dated 12 April 1912
Cameron, Stephen, *Titanic: Belfast's Own*, 1998
Cedar Rapids Evening Gazette for 16 January 1914
Census Returns, 1841-1911
Chicago Daily Journal for 19 April 1912 and 16 January 1914
Chirnside, Mark, *The 'Olympic' Class Ships*, 2004
Cleveland Plain Dealer for 19 April 1912
Cooper, G J, *Titanic Captain: The Life of Edward John Smith*, 2011
Cumberland and Westmoreland Herald for 20 April 1912
Daily Sketch for 9 May 1912
Davenport-Hines, Richard, *Titanic Lives: Migrants and Millionaires, Conmen and Crew*, 2012
Encyclopaedia Titanica
Everett, Marshall, *Wreck and Sinking of Titanic, the Oceans Greatest Disaster*, 1912
Findmypast
Geller, Judith B, *Titanic: Women and Children First*, 1998
Gracie, Archibald, *The Truth about Titanic*, 1973
Hampshire Advertiser for 14 February 1914
Harland and Wolff Director's Minute Book held in the Public Records Office

Herts Advertiser and St Albans Times for 4 May 1912
Holman, Hannah, *Titanic Voices: 63 Survivors Tell Their Extraordinary Stories*, 2011
Hume, Yvonne and Hume, John Law, and Dean, Millvina, *RMS Titanic: The First Violin; the True Story of Titanic's First Violinist*
Hyslop, Donald; Forsyth, Alastair; Jemima, Sheila, *Titanic Voices: Memories from the Fateful Voyage*, 1994
Ilford Graphic for 19 April 1912 and 10 May 1912
Jessop, Violet and Maxtone-Graham, John, *The Memoirs of Violet Jessop, Stewardess*, 1998
Julian, Hester: *Memorials of Henry Forbes Julian*, 1914
JWB Historical Library, the
Lightoller, Charles Herbert, *Titanic and Other Ships*, 1935
Liverpool Echo for 18 March 1913
Lord, Walter, *A Night to Remember*, 1955
Lord, Walter, *The Night Lives On: Thoughts, Theories and Revelations about Titanic*, 1986
Lowell Sun (Masachsetts) for 28 May 1912
Marion Weekly Star (Ohio) for 27 April 1912
Manchester Evening News for 14 April 1912, 18 April 1912 and 16 April 1917
Merseyside Maritime Museum
Moss, Michael S and John R Hume, *Shipbuilders to the World: 125 Years of Harland and Wolf, Belfast, 1861-1986*, 1986
Myers, L T, *The Sinking of Titanic and Great Sea Disasters* 1912
National Archives
National Maritime Museum
Navratil, Elizabeth, *Survivors: A True Life Titanic Story*, 1999
Newcastle Morning Herald for 15 April 1913
Newport Daily News for 19 April 1912
New York Herald for 21 April 1912
New York Times for 19 April 1912; 21 April 1912; 8 July 1912
New York World for 21 April 1912
North Devon Journal for 25 April 1912
Nottingham Evening Post for 28 May 1914
Oldham, Wilton J, *The Ismay Line: The White Star Line and the Ismay Family Story*, 1961
Oxford Times for 27 April 1912
Padfield, Peter, *Titanic and the Californian*, 1965
Portsmouth Evening News of 10 February 1914
Rostron, Sir Arthur Henry, *Home from the Sea*, 1931
Russell, Gareth, *The Ship of Dreams: The Sinking of Titanic and the End of the Edwardian Era*, 2019
Salford City Council, Births, Deaths and Marriages
Sheffield Daily Independent for 4 May 1912
Sheil, Inger, *Titanic Valour: The Life of Fifth Officer Harold Lowe*, 2012
Smith, Corporal William, *The Wreck of the Troopship Birkenhead, 1852, (The) Royal Magazine*, 1905

Society of Naval Architects and Marine Engineers, *Titanic: The Anatomy of a Disaster: A Report from the Marine Forensic Panel*, 1997
Southampton Times and Hampshire Express for 18 May 1912
Southport Guardian for 17 April 1912 and 20 April 1912
Southport Visitor for 18 April 1912 and 20 April 1912
Stenson, Patrick, *Titanic Voyage: The Odyssey of C H Lightoller*, 1998
Stevens Point Journal, Wisconsin for 27 April 1912
Stringer, Craig, *Titanic People*, 2012
Sun, the New York for 17 January 1914
Ticehurst, Brian, *Titanic's Rescuers: Captain, Sir Arthur Rostron and the Crew of the* Carpathia, 1996
Times, the for 17 January 1914
Titanic Commutator, The Journal of Titanic Historical Society
Titanic Historical Society
Titanic International Society
Toronto Daily Star for 28 August 1912
Turner, Steve, *The Band That Played On: The Extraordinary Story of the 8 Musicians Who Went Down With Titanic*, 2011
United States Enquiry, *Investigation into the Loss of the SS Titanic*, 1912
Ward, Christopher, *And the Band Played On: Titanic Violinist and the Glovemaker, A True Story of Love, Loss and Betrayal*, 2011
Welshman, Dr John, *Titanic: The Last Night of a Small Town*, 2012
Washington Herald for 21 April 1912
Washington Post for 21 April 1912
Washington Times for 19 April 1912
Western Daily Mercury for 30 April 1912
Whitehaven News for 2 May 1912
Whiteley, Thomas, *Titanic Lecture*
Wilson, Andrew, *Shadow of Titanic: The Extraordinary Stories of Those Who Survived*, 2012
Winocour, Jack, *The Story of Titanic, as told by its Survivors*, 1960
Worcestershire Villager for April/May 2012
Yorkshire Post and Leeds Intelligencer for 16 August 1922

Index